THE POLITICS OF THE MINIMUM WAGE

THE POLITICS
OF THE MINIMUM WAGE

Jerold Waltman

University of Illinois Press

Urbana and Chicago

Library of Congress Cataloging-in-Publication Data
Waltman, Jerold L., 1945–
The politics of the minimum wage / Jerold Waltman.
p.   cm.
Includes bibliographical references and index.
ISBN 0-252-02545-8 (alk. paper)
1. Minimum wage—United States. I. Title.
HD4918.W265   2000
331.2'3—dc21   99-6830
CIP

C 5 4 3 2 1

To my coworkers at A & W Root Beer,
Ruston, Louisiana, 1963–67

Except perhaps for the Social Security Act, it is the most far-reaching, far-sighted program for the benefit of workers ever adopted here or in any other country.

—Franklin D. Roosevelt, 1938

It constitutes a step in the direction of communism, bolshevism, fascism, and Nazism.

—National Association of Manufacturers, 1937

I think we ought to add the millennium to the program. Otherwise, it will not be complete.

—Senator Josiah Bailey (D–N.C.), 1938

The most surprising day ever seen in this place was yesterday when the boss was ordered to pay us the code rate. . . . You can guess the money is handy. But there is something more than the money. There is knowing that the working man don't stand alone against the bosses and their smart lawyers and all their tricks. There is a government now that cares whether things is fair for us. I tell you that is more than money. It gives you a good feeling instead of all the time burning up because nothing is fair.

—A New England textile worker, 1935 (referring to the minimum wage section of the National Industrial Recovery Act)

CONTENTS

Preface *xi*

Introduction *1*

1. The Politics of Ideas 9
2. A Brief Political History through 1989 28
3. Public Opinion 48
4. The Sociology of the Minimum Wage 69
5. Policy-Making: Raising the Minimum Wage in 1996 89
6. Impact and Feedback 108

Conclusion 135

Notes 147

Index 169

My interest in the minimum wage began during my undergraduate years, when I worked at two jobs. One was at a small restaurant, to which the minimum wage did not apply. I began at less than half the minimum wage and after five years had risen to 60 percent of that level. About half the workers were college students, some with serious financial needs but a number simply earning a little extra money. For all of the students, though, it was only a temporary situation. For the other half, however, this job was their livelihood. There was the woman whose husband was a motel maintenance worker, the wife of the disabled sawmill worker, the middle-aged single mother, and others. These are the people whose faces I have never forgotten and to whom this book is dedicated.

The owner, a truly self-made businessman with an acute intelligence but only an elementary school education, would come out from time to time and chat with the carhops. He frequently vowed, no doubt sincerely, that if the minimum wage was ever applied to fast-food establishments, it would destroy the industry. The economics I was studying at the time seemed to support that view. However, I kept thinking there must be some way to elevate the incomes of those permanently employed at the A & W Root Beer stands of the world and still maintain the viability of business enterprises.

At my other job, I sold office supplies and printing. One day a customer, a lumberyard owner, was ruminating on the minimum wage. I wish, he said, that the minimum wage applied to my business. I would like to pay my workers more, but the competitive nature of this business makes it difficult to raise wages above a certain level. If the law applied to everybody, it would make for a level playing field. He added that if his workers' wages were higher, they could also afford better homes, which would use more lumber. Wouldn't everyone be better off then? he asked rhetorically. It seemed to me then, and still seems now, that there is as much wisdom there as in the graphs that pepper every introductory economics textbook.

This is not a book, however, about the economics of the minimum wage, although economic ideas and arguments inevitably intrude. It is a book about politics, particularly political ideas. In the search for the roots of public policies, political scientists often come close to embracing mechanistic explanations: that policies derive from social and economic structures or political and institutional factors almost by osmosis. Public policies, however, are designed by human beings who are motivated and limited by the ideas they carry around in their heads. How political elites and public intellectuals think about public issues therefore goes far to shape the contours of public policy. I have sought to elaborate the ideas participants in the minimum wage debate have historically brought and bring today to the political arena and connect these ideas to broader themes in political and social theory.

At the same time, I am seeking to do more than analyze. I am critical of both sides of the minimum wage divide. Although I would like to think that I could somehow strike a nerve that would move the free market fundamentalists among us closer to the position that markets are instrumental rather than theological arrangements, I have little hope of doing so. Instead, I address much of the prescriptive thrust of what follows to those I have called social welfare liberals. When called on to defend the minimum wage, they turn primarily to two arguments: (1) that it does not do much if any harm and (2) that it is a useful, if modest, adjunct to cash transfer programs, such as the Earned Income Tax Credit. My goal is to provide the material that will put the case for the minimum wage in a more positive fashion and elevate its importance. In that endeavor, I have some hope.

It is a pleasure to acknowledge those who have helped bring this book to fruition. Many scholars and colleagues have contributed to my thinking throughout the years, but David Robertson of the University of Missouri–St. Louis deserves a special note of thanks. He and I have discussed labor market policies for years, and he has always brought incisive ideas to the table. Daniel Hamermesh of the University of Texas was gracious enough to give me a helpful critique of chapter 6, even though he disagrees with most of what is there. Ronald King of Tulane hosted a presentation on the book's thesis and proved a superb source of ideas. Two anonymous reviewers for the University of Illinois Press provided especially insightful and thought-provoking commentary. Richard Martin at the University of Illinois Press exemplifies all that an academic editor should be and has been more than a pleasure to work with. The production staff at the press has guided the technical end of things in a most salutary and efficient manner. A special nod goes to Jane Mohraz for her copyediting.

A number of librarians bore up well under my barrage of requests for documents and reports of various sorts. Of these, Eleanor Robin at the University of Southern Mississippi was especially invaluable. Also, the staff at the Bureau of Labor Statistics responded quickly and courteously to my e-mails and phone calls. A sabbatical leave during the fall of 1997 provided an opportunity to do research without interruption. Ronald Marquardt, chair of the Department of Political Science; Glenn T. Harper, dean of the College of Liberal Arts; and Donald Cotten, the vice-president for research at the University of Southern Mississippi, all provided needed funds and help at critical junctures. Finally, my family suffered the inevitable preoccupation and absences that come with writing a book, and I am grateful for their forbearance.

THE POLITICS OF THE MINIMUM WAGE

This book explains and evaluates the politics of the federal minimum wage program. I argue that even though the minimum wage is an economic regulatory policy, a politics of symbolism more than anything else defines the political contests that periodically erupt over it. I also show that the political economy of citizenship deserves to stand alongside the economic arguments that now dominate the minimum wage debate. More detail on the critique is provided in chapter 1, after I lay out the original ideas that led to a minimum wage and trace their evolution. For now, I concentrate on the explanatory side, setting out some notes on symbolic politics and placing them within the larger framework of policy theory.

For many years, political scientists spent most of their time analyzing the political process. Careful case studies focused on the interplay of interest groups, political parties, legislative committees, the president, and a variety of other actors. The result of political activity, the statute or administrative order, was viewed exclusively as a dependent variable. Politics perforce determined the content of public policy.

In a justifiably famous 1964 article, Theodore J. Lowi insightfully turned this proposition around. It was the character of policies, he argued, that determined political patterns, because particular policies have certain attributes that lead policymakers to behave in different ways.[1] He initially identified what have since become the three familiar types: distributive policies, regulatory policies, and redistributive policies. Distributive policies are those marked by the "ease with which they can be disaggregated and dispensed unit by small unit, each unit more or less in isolation from any general rule."[2] Regulatory policies are largely self-explanatory, encompassing commands to do or not to do some act, ordinarily "directly raising costs and/or reducing or expanding the al-

ternatives of private individuals."[3] Redistributive policies involve transfers of resources, with identifiable winners and losers.

Distributive policies spawn a politics of "pork barrel" and "logroll-
ing." Each claimant wants a piece of the whole, and no one need lose
if others obtain their bit. Regulatory politics are pluralistic, with shifting coalitions of interest groups, low levels of ideological conflict, and
pragmatic bargaining and compromise. Redistributive policies, in
contrast, trigger ideological and class-based politics.

Lowi has subsequently elaborated and refined the schema, without
altering its fundamental thrust. In 1972, he added a fourth category,
constituent policy, the domain of internal governmental structure, such
as reapportionment and executive reorganization.[4] Writing in 1988, he
expanded the framework even further.[5] First, he divided the four areas
into mainstream and radicalized versions. Quite logically, he contended
that politics takes on a different hue if an issue area moves from the
mainstream to the radical. In the area of regulatory policy, for instance,
he says that "error" becomes "sin." Next, he divided the radical category under each rubric into "left" and "right" versions. Inasmuch as
the piece was drafted as a foreword to a book on "social regulatory
policy"—with chapters on school prayer, pornography, crime, gun control, affirmative action, and abortion—the emphasis was on the distinction between regulating conduct that has merely undesirable consequences (error) and behavior deemed harmful in itself (sin). In the latter
instance, politics is likely to be infused with moral overtones, and its
style bleeds over into the redistributive. Ideological intensity and morally conditioned single interest groups tend to become the rule.

Robert Spitzer has attempted to defend the scheme against some of
its critics by reconstituting the model along two dimensions, the "ap-
plicability of coercion" and the "likelihood of coercion."[6] The former
refers to whether the coercion is aimed at the individual or the general environment, the latter to how remote or immediate the threat is.
He then locates each of the four types of policy in one of the quad-
rants but bifurcates each by a diagonal line. The four diagonal lines
then form a square within the original box. The central point is that
in each area there are policies that have a politics approaching each

of the other categories. We therefore have pure and mixed cases of each policy type, along with their accompanying politics.

Two basic premises underlie both Lowi's recent writing and Spitzer's efforts. First, they emphasize the coercive element in public policy. Lowi defines public policy "simply as an officially expressed intention backed up by a sanction"; therefore, "all policies must be understood as coercive."[7] Likewise, Spitzer utilizes coercion as the defining characteristic of his typology. Second, they stress that the policy classification determined by the analyst, not the perceptions of the participants, controls the type of politics that ensues. "Policies are categorized," Spitzer says, "according to the wording and interpretation found in the statute itself, not according to the perceptions of the actors involved."[8] I take issue with the first premise because it seems to me unnecessarily narrow and with the second because I think it would be better stated as a fruitful source of hypotheses, two points to which I return momentarily.

Two other scholars have offered thoughtful additions to Lowi's model. James L. Anderson used early twentieth-century public health policy to argue that "governmental suasion" was an area that deserved attention.[9] Lowi responded that suasion was better seen as an enforcement strategy for regulatory and redistributive policy rather than as a new category.[10] Anderson replied that he was not trying to create a new category but was only suggesting "that thinking that policies rest solely upon the coercive power of government lacks the breadth we need to understand the nature of governing."[11]

T. Alexander Smith applied the framework in a comparative context but added a fourth category of his own, "emotive symbolic" policies.[12] Influenced by James B. Christoph's study of the termination of capital punishment in Great Britain,[13] Smith demonstrated the real political conflicts that frequently emerge from struggles over symbols. His examples included the European army debate in France, civil rights in the United States, and the flag dispute in Canada.

I am in accord with James L. Anderson's position that an exclusive focus on coercion fails to capture the range of public policies and hence political activity we observe around us. Take Lowi's constituent policy category, for example. When a state moves its presidential primary from one date to another, is there really any coercion involved? Moreover, there are many governmental decisions of the type that Smith discussed. When the Georgia legislature voted to retain the confederate symbol on its state flag or when Congress added "under God" to the Pledge of Allegiance, coercion was all but invisible. Surely these decisions are public policies, broadly defined. The anthropologist Simon Harrison has developed a detailed four-fold classification of such contests over political symbolism, and none of them can readily be accommodated within the Lowi framework.[14] Finally, while some suasive policies have implicit coercion behind them (the "Just Say No" campaign to discourage drug use, for example), others seem more purely suasive (the effort to encourage the use of condoms, for instance).

I hesitate to suggest modifying any aspect of Lowi's scheme. But if a richer reality can be viewed with a modification and, more important, interesting theory can be generated, it is worth the effort. I propose that we define public policy as any statute or administrative act adopted by the appropriate legal authority.[15] We can then divide policies into coercive and noncoercive categories (see figure 1). This actually restores much of Lowi's original scheme, because it removes constituent policies from the initial grouping. This rubric never actually seemed to fit comfortably within the framework, and neither Lowi nor those who applied his scheme have devoted much attention to it. Suasive and symbolic policies then flesh out the scheme and give it a certain symmetry.

Next is the matter of classification by researcher versus how the participants may see matters. Aynsley Kellow argued the case for relying on the views of the participants, as Lowi did originally.[16] Relying on E. E. Schattschneider, Kellow stressed how important it is for

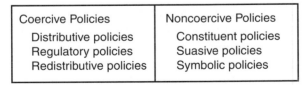

Coercive Policies	Noncoercive Policies
Distributive policies	Constituent policies
Regulatory policies	Suasive policies
Redistributive policies	Symbolic policies

Figure 1. A Revised Policy Typology

political contestants to be able to define the issues under debate. Lowi called Kellow's effort "a brilliant piece" but maintained that perceptions of the policymakers "count, but are secondary to the 'nature' of the proposals or formal policies themselves. [Once a] definition is in fact fixed in the proposal or the policy, it will shape the form of participation, *no matter how participants 'perceive' it.*"[17]

Could we not clarify this matter by stating that as a testable hypothesis? That is, if an informed observer, reading the proposal or statute, assigns a case to the regulatory category, say, while a study of the members of Congress involved demonstrates that they viewed it as redistributive, is it not an empirical question which was dominant, or controlling, in shaping the political process? It would seem at least arguable that the objective character of the policy versus the participants' perception is better seen as a variable rather than as a deciding factor in a classification scheme. If so, we can expand the framework another step, resulting in each policy's being categorized twice. A number of quite interesting theoretical propositions could then be generated and tested when the two diverge.

The pages that follow demonstrate that both these distinctions help us grasp contemporary minimum wage politics. On the surface, the minimum wage law is a standard regulatory policy. A statute explicitly states that any business or other entity employing a covered worker must pay the person at least a minimum wage. The threat of coercion—back-pay awards and fines—awaits any violators. In fact, Raymond Tatalovich and Byron Daynes cite it as a typical example of a regulatory policy in the introductory essay to their book.[18]

According to Lowi's formulations, regulatory policies should produce a politics of pluralism.[19] However, pluralism is hardly what is revealed in the following chapters. Rather than pragmatic bargaining, we see a politics based largely on ideology and symbolism. This means that the theoretical linkages forged by the framework are awry, the minimum wage is a special case, or the classification scheme needs modification/elaboration. The third alternative seems the most plausible and drawing a distinction between the analyst's and the participants' perceptions appears a reasonable course to pursue in accomplishing that.

The symbolic aspects of minimum wage politics, however, are quite different from the examples discussed by T. Alexander Smith. His emotive symbolic politics bore four characteristics: (1) a wide scope and intense level of conflict over "way of life" issues; (2) ordinary legislators, backed by groups with a moral agenda, rather than leaders playing a major role; (3) little party discipline; and (4) policy being made in the legislature, with a high degree of individualism among legislators.[20] The third and fourth can be found, more or less, in American minimum wage politics. It is the first and second features, though, that largely set apart the kind of emotive symbolic issues Smith analyzed, typified more than anything by the Canadian flag dispute. Rather than a wide scope and an intense conflict, we encounter an issue with quite low salience among citizens. The conflict is momentarily intense to a number of policymakers, as it is fought out by members of Congress, the president, and a small coterie of intellectuals and policy analysts. The issue ignites strong feelings among a few faithful, but the public is largely unmoved, even though its preferences are clear. Instead of single purpose, morally oriented groups, we discover groups with only passing interest. Minimum wage proposals trigger a flurry of interest group activity, to be sure, with both business groups and unions taking predictable stances and rehearsing well-worn symbolic arguments. As soon as the vote is taken, though, both sets of groups turn immediately to more pressing and more practical matters. In short, they return to issues where pluralism is the dominant form of politics.

We therefore cannot understand minimum wage politics without creating a category for symbolic politics and disentangling an objective classification of policy types from how the matter is seen by the participants. The first is necessary because the type of politics we observe in this area does not fit with what the framework would predict, a politics of pluralism. The second flows from the fact that how people involved in a policy-making decision see an issue goes far in determining how they act, and how these people act surely affects the texture of political activity.

The conclusion stresses, but it bears noting here, that it is important also to distinguish among the various types of symbolic politics and their related policies. Merely because the politics of a policy area is heavily influenced by symbolism does not mean that the policy itself is without tangible impact. Certain types of symbolic politics may well produce policies that have only emotional consequences. Putting "In God We Trust" on our coins may make people feel good or bad, but the money is worth the same. In contrast, the politics of capital punishment in Britain may have been emotive and symbolic, but for those convicted of murder the outcome of the decision was anything but symbolic. Similarly, the politics of the minimum wage may be laden with symbolism, but for minimum wage workers and their employers the consequences of a yes or no vote are quite real.

1

The Politics of Ideas

All public policies rest on two layers of ideas. At the most basic level lie those fundamental, unspoken assumptions that are the glue of any society. These influence public policy by forming a boundary around what is acceptable, containing politics and political action within limited confines. At a more immediate level, there is the thinking that public officials and those who actively follow public affairs bring to everyday politics. Proposals that end up as public policies do not simply materialize from thin air. They are the product of someone's specific ideas about how a public problem should be handled.

While the outcomes of the continual jousts that make up the grist of politics in every democratic capital are affected by many factors, the ideas behind what is being discussed remain critically important. How problems are defined and what concrete proposals are advanced to address the situation strongly influence the shape of public programs. Moreover, once on the statute books, public policies are seldom if ever static, either in their operation or in the politics surrounding them. Since political coalitions and the ideas on which they are based change over time, the same policy may exhibit strikingly different political dynamics from one time period to another.

Many features of American minimum wage politics have remained largely constant. The positions of those who opposed the adoption of minimum wage laws when they were first introduced late in the nineteenth century are recognizable variations on the themes continually repeated by opponents today. There are, however, important differences. Supporters of the minimum wage have undergone a significant metamorphosis, as they have cast aside many of the earlier justifications for a minimum wage and substituted others in their stead.

Contemporary social welfare liberals, the principal backers of the minimum wage, have abandoned a number of the precepts of both

Progressivism and the New Deal when it comes to the minimum wage. Progressivism was important because it initiated and incubated the idea, while the New Deal was responsible for securing adoption of the federal minimum wage in 1938. Both of these stories are interesting and worth telling, but the philosophical distance separating today's minimum wage partisans from their Progressive ancestors is of deeper significance. Progressivism retained a link with an earlier civic republican tradition, in which political economy included issues of citizenship. Modern social welfare liberals, in contrast, have firmly rooted themselves in the individualist strand of American political thought, thereby altering the context in which they see the relationship between economics and politics.

We have arrived at a point when the vacuity that an extreme individualist political philosophy inevitably breeds has forced us to dust off civic republican ideas on a wide variety of fronts. If we end up moving toward a revived civic republicanism, the minimum wage is quite likely to be one of the prime policy areas that will undergo a decided change in its politics.

Our first task is to examine the Progressive heritage of the minimum wage; our second is to take a quick tour of contemporary minimum wage politics. Finally, we will look at how a political economy of citizenship might redefine those politics.

Progressivism

The existence of a legal minimum wage in the United States is directly traceable to Progressivism, the broad movement for social and political reform that flowered in the years before World War I. It was Progressives who first laid the intellectual foundations necessary for a minimum wage to even secure a hearing. Without their reorientation of American public philosophy, any hope of seeing a minimum wage enacted in this country would have been dim indeed. Second, identifiable Progressives imported the idea of the minimum wage from abroad and mounted the political pressure to push the first such law through the Massachusetts legislature. Had it not been for these people's dedication and determination, there would have been little prospect of an American minimum wage, either at the state level or at the federal level.

The world's first minimum wage was adopted by the Australian state of Victoria in 1896.[1] The law did not provide for a uniform minimum wage for all workers but instead established a wage board that was empowered to set basic wages for six industries that habitually paid low wages. Slated as a four-year experiment, it was renewed and expanded in 1900 and then made permanent in 1904. By that time, its reach encompassed 150 different industries. The other Australian states and New Zealand passed similar legislation within a few years, and Great Britain followed suit in 1909.

It fell to an organization called the National Consumers' League (NCL) to serve as the impetus for American legislation.[2] In 1890, a group of affluent women in New York, concerned about the deplorable conditions in many of that city's sweatshops, determined to do something about it. Sweatshops, small manufacturing sites where people, often young women, worked long hours in unhealthy and dangerous environments for extremely low wages, characterized much of the clothing, candy-making, box-manufacturing, and other trades. The reformers decided to found the Consumers' League of the City of New York, made up of women like themselves who would avoid purchasing items not manufactured in accordance with a code of "fair house" standards that they had drawn up. They hoped that such commercial pressure would at least ameliorate the worst of the sweatshop conditions. Other consumers' leagues soon sprang up in Massachusetts, Pennsylvania, and Illinois, and in 1899 they joined together to form a national organization.

Progress was excruciatingly slow, however, since these women represented only a small minority of consumers. Moreover, trying to set up a mechanism to inspect factories to be certain they were abiding by the code proved a daunting task. It was an exasperated and disheartened group of NCL leaders who went to a conference on sweatshops in Geneva in 1908. There they heard presentations and reports on the operation of the Australasian minimum wage laws and came home believers. They persuaded the NCL's board of directors in 1909 to endorse a legally mandated minimum wage for women. The reason for confining the proposal to women was partly philosophical; some of their allies in the Progressive movement felt men should not be made the objects of paternalistic legislation. Mostly, though, the reason was tactical. The Supreme Court was still adhering to doctrines that stressed liberty of contract, but it had recently upheld an Oregon statute setting maximum hours for women.[3] The chief argument Oregon had used was that women are different from men and need the state's protection to ensure their health. There was no guarantee, of course, that the Supreme Court would extend this logic to a minimum wage law. However, it was almost certain that any law covering both men and women would have been struck down.[4]

The NCL's leaders enlisted the help of Felix Frankfurter, then a professor at the Harvard Law School, and began a campaign in Massachusetts. In 1912, they managed to muster enough support in the legislature to pass the nation's first minimum wage law, although it was a largely toothless statute. The story of the subsequent spread of state minimum wage laws and the origins of the federal law will be picked up in the next chapter. For now, we turn our attention to the ideas that made possible the political reception of the minimum wage.

Had there been no Progressive intellectual movement to reshape how many in the political elite saw the world, the minimum wage would have found barren soil. Even if the members of the NCL had been enthralled by and dedicated to securing a minimum wage, it would have received no serious consideration.

Progressivism is one of those historical movements that cut such a broad swath across American history that it cannot be neatly defined or even assigned a pair of dates.[5] Some historians have even suggested we jettison the term entirely.[6] Nevertheless, for all its vagueness, its cross-currents, and even its contradictions, a general outline can be sketched. For our purposes, there were four elements of Progressivism that are most germane.

First, Progressives were willing to come to grips with the new industrial and urban society. Unlike the Populists, who largely fought a quasi-Luddite battle against industrialization, the Progressives accepted it as part of a normal historical evolution. What they sought were ways to tame it and make it more humane. Second, there was a strong religious dimension to Progressivism. The Social Gospel, based mostly in the mainline Protestant churches, was an intimate part of Progressivism.[7] In Eldon Eisenach's study of nineteen prominent Progressives, all but one of them had strong religious roots in upscale Protestant denominations.[8] Third, Progressives had a deep affinity for the nation and the idea of community. They also accepted the political corollary that a public good exists apart from the mere summation of individual interests. John R. Commons and John B. Andrews wrote in 1916, "Hence it is that every act of the legislature must be tested by a standard which shall determine whether the persons or classes of persons to be benefited are so benefited merely because they have power in the legislature to impose burdens on others, or because the benefit to them is also a benefit to that body of the whole people which we call 'the public.'"[9] In the same vein, James Kloppenberg noted that the philosopher William James "denied the liberal contention that the pursuit of personal interest insures optimal social benefit. The public interest, like the ethical ideal, emerges from the concrete struggles among competing conceptions of the good."[10] Fourth, Progressives had an inductive epistemology. They believed that knowledge accrued by examining the world as it is and people's relations in actual situations. Armed with these observations, the social scientist could advance generalizations, tentative hypotheses that could be subsequently tested against other information and new data.

Many Progressives were academic political economists, since the immense changes engendered by industrialization seemed to beg for analysis and understanding. Political economists of this generation turned away from the older deductive political economy of Adam Smith, David Ricardo, and Thomas Malthus.[11] These earlier thinkers had constructed an elaborate model of economic theory, called classical economics, which they argued had the status of natural law.[12] The propositions deduced from the model were true regardless of time or space. If an individual or government violated one of the precepts, it was as if the law of gravity were violated; the consequences were swift, certain, and unpleasant. For the resulting grim outlook on human affairs, it was popularly dubbed the "dismal science." Progressive political economists rejected this approach. Instead, they turned to what they called the historical and comparative method. The proper way to analyze economic life is to examine what people are doing, not to formulate propositions from a theoretical model and declare them valid. Economic laws might therefore vary from place to place and from time to time. Even the "law" of supply and demand, they held, is culturally grounded. Quoting the renowned Belgian economist Emile de Laveleye with approval, Richard T. Ely pointed out that fish could be scarce and cheap if a religious prohibition kept people from eating fish.[13]

Progressive political economy also harbored a strong religious element. Sidney Fine has documented, for example, that nearly half of the founding members of the American Economic Association were clergymen.[14] The study of economics was therefore undertaken not just for the intellectual satisfaction it brought. Its more important goal was to serve God by finding ways to make the world a more just place. Many of these people wrote regularly on religious matters in addition to economics, and references to God and the need to work his will crop up throughout their writings.

Markets were generally viewed with favor, though as merely a human institution through which efficiencies were achieved, not as a deified phenomenon unalterable by human agency. A few of them, it is true, flirted with mild versions of socialism from time to time, but their basic preference for markets persevered.[15] They believed that government action could make markets work better. When bargaining power between two parties was grossly unequal or when monopolies raised prices, there was no real market. Government therefore had a moral obligation to insert itself into these situations to correct for market failure.

All these aspects of Progressivism featured prominently in their writings on the minimum wage.[16] Almost every discussion began with a catalog of what it would take for a worker and his family or a single woman, in some cases, to lead a minimally decent life. Of course, some of the tabulations differed in what they put in or left out, but the idea was always the same. They often quoted with approval the Australian standard: a minimum wage is one supporting "the normal needs of the average employee regarded as a human being living in a civilized community."[17] They then proceeded to show through statistics provided by various reports and investigations how many people fell below the standard, always a sobering if not staggering number. Summarizing the findings, Arthur Holcombe said, "In the light of these and other recent investigations into the standard of living among the industrial population of the United States, the fact that a very considerable number of workpeople are now employed in the United States at less than an American standard-of-living wage may be regarded as sufficiently established."[18] The religious and statistical strands in Progressivism thus coalesced.

Most Progressives who wrestled with the question of industrial organization concluded that unions were the best hope for raising wages generally. By engaging in collective bargaining, they could mitigate somewhat the disparity between owners and workers. However, they called attention to the special barriers that inhibited the organizing of low-wage workers into unions, whether they were the transient female department store clerks or the desperate immigrants herded into factories and mills. A minimum wage was the only practical way to secure for them anything above a subsistence livelihood. Morality commanded a decent living for all; practicality made the minimum wage the most workable answer.

They were certainly not unaware of the objections opponents raised, objections that were largely the same ones voiced today: unemployment, business failures, inflation, and, in the case of state laws, the possibility that companies would simply relocate to states without minimum wage laws.[19] The unemployment argument was countered by insisting, first, that there were often excess profits, above normal returns to land, capital, and management that could be used to pay higher wages. Second, they suggested that a minimum wage would force inefficient managements to reorder their production processes, to the benefit of the whole society. The business failure argument drew the most interesting response. Firms that paid starvation wages, they contended, were actually drawing on society's wealth to stay in business. They were shifting part of the cost of doing business to hospitals, soup kitchens, and other charitable organizations. Even with the low price of the goods, society therefore loses. "Not until an industry has developed the ingenuity, the incentive, and organizing ability, to make it self-sustaining in all of its returns, ought society to have that industry," averred George Groat.[20] In short, added Arthur Holcombe, "Such industries as these, the country is better without."[21]

As for rising prices, they calculated how small a percentage labor costs are in most firms' total cost picture and how tiny an amount prices would have to rise even if the entire minimum wage was passed on to the consumer. The final objection was met by maintaining that heavy investments in fixed assets made it unlikely businesses would pack up and move to save a few dollars in wage costs. They also stressed that after Victoria adopted its law, there was only one business that cited minimum wage costs in its decision to move elsewhere. (Then, by poetic justice, the state to which it moved enacted a minimum wage law.) Commons and Andrews, pointing to Australia and New Zealand, put it succinctly: "From the side of employers it is frequently declared that minimum wage laws will put them under such a handicap that they will be forced to move to freer territory or be driven out of industry altogether. Neither seems to have taken place to any appreciable extent."[22] Or, more generally: "It is still alleged in some quarters that wages are fixed by economic laws, any legislative interference with which can result only in disaster. At present all that can be said is that the experience covering twenty years in Victoria and shorter periods elsewhere has failed to confirm these dire predictions."[23]

Minimum wage advocates made two additional points. One was that when workers received a minimum wage, it implied productive, disciplined work. The minimum wage was a way not only to provide a decent income but also to give a dignity to work; but if workers did not respond, there would be little sympathy. The prominent Progressive Herbert Croly cautioned, "They [wage earners] must be worth their salt. Insofar as they are not worth their salt, they must be helped, trained and sometimes coerced to become so."[24] The other was that they freely acknowledged a minimum wage would leave some people unemployable. Those who were physically or mentally unable to produce enough to justify employers' granting the minimum wage would have to be cared for by public provision in a humane and dignified way. They should not be forced, as they were under the present system, to toil for whatever pittance they could obtain, with ruinous results for themselves and other workers. After the adoption of a minimum wage, the state must take responsibility for all who "cannot be and should not be required to be self-supporting."[25] What they seemed to have in mind was the provision of services, not a cash transfer program.[26]

A survey of Progressivism and the minimum wage is not complete without mentioning Father John Ryan. An economist who taught at a Catholic seminary, he wrote the most comprehensive treatise on the subject.[27] Although his Catholic roots placed him at some distance from the mainstream of the movement, he was deeply involved in the activities of a number of Progressive organizations. Ryan based his argument on Catholic concepts of natural law and the church's social teachings, particularly as enunciated in Pope Leo XIII's 1891 encyclical *Rerum Novarum*.[28] The right to a living wage, Ryan argued, was among the natural rights possessed by people simply as creatures of God. The right, as all rights, of course, had to be tempered in practice to the extent that it infringed on other rights. The central questions were whether it impinged too deeply on property rights and, if not, how best to secure it. His positions were that it did not do the former and that state action was the only feasible route for the latter. Because his generalizations were fairly sweeping—in that he extended coverage to men as well as women and to workers in every sector of the economy—and because he grounded the policy in a natural right to a living wage, many Progressives were not willing to follow along on his road.

Contemporary Divisions over the Minimum Wage

Contemporary minimum wage politics is characterized largely by symbolism and ideology. There is, however, an asymmetrical relationship between the two. To the opponents of minimum wage increases, who often also oppose the whole concept of a minimum wage, it is both ideological and symbolic. To its proponents, it is equally symbolic, but it lacks a parallel ideological component.

The members of Congress, denizens of such think tanks as the Cato Institute, the Heritage Foundation, and the American Enterprise Institute, and sympathetic academics and journalists who most ardently oppose the minimum wage worship at the altar of free market fundamentalism. Intellectually, they are followers of Milton Friedman and his acolytes, actual or vicarious members of the "Chicago school" of economists.[29] Friedman's two most widely read works are *Capitalism and Freedom* and *Free to Choose*, both of which stress the sanctity of individual economic choice.[30]

In *Capitalism and Freedom*, he wrote, "Economic arrangements play a dual role in the promotion of a free society. On the one hand, freedom in economic arrangements is itself a component of freedom broadly understood, so economic freedom is an end in itself. In the second place, economic freedom is also an indispensable means toward the achievement of political freedom."[31] Later, he said simply that "freedom of the individual, or perhaps the family, is our ultimate goal in judging social arrangements."[32] In *Free to Choose*, he argued that an economic bill of rights was needed to enshrine the market system into fundamental law. One of the provisions of his proposal reads, "Congress shall make no laws abridging the freedom of sellers of goods or labor to price their products or services."[33]

In short, to Friedman and his followers, the market and justice are synonymous. If the market assigns a certain value to a good or service, then it has that value, objectively and morally. To be sure, almost every market fundamentalist draws a line somewhere concerning aspects of life that should not be subject to market transactions, but these domains tend to be precious few.[34] Manifestly, when it comes to labor—people selling their services for a wage—they see absolutely no difference between a labor market and markets for pizzas, shoes, hammers, or automobiles. If an employer is willing to pay me a given amount to work for eight hours and I accept, we must both be better off than we were before the transaction. A market price has thus been set as surely as when a farmer brings a bushel of tomatoes to market.

The great power of this extreme form of neoclassical economics is that it is both a science and a religion. It has a timeless framework based on natural laws. At the same time, it predicts exactly how the world works. Logically, of course, one should not be allowed to have it both ways.[35] If the system is a science, it needs to be subject to invalidation through the ordinary process of inquiry. There are really only two ways to go about disconfirming such a model: show the assumptions on which it is built to be false or demonstrate that the hypotheses generated by it do not accord with reality. The first can be circumvented if one is prepared to rely on the power of the propositions. That is, if the model is predictively powerful, it may not be relevant that the assumptions are simplifications or even false. Market fundamentalists, however, have not been noticeably eager to reexamine their model when reality stubbornly refuses to go along with their predictions, as we see in chapter 6. If the system is a religion, entirely different standards apply. The evaluative criteria should be drawn from philosophy and theology, and it must be laid alongside other value systems and judged accordingly. In the meantime, though, if one claims to have found the key to both normative and empirical truth, these criticisms do not register. Consequently, to its adherents, free market fundamentalism remains both inspiring and irrefutable.

In a way that few other policies do, the minimum wage offends free market fundamentalism. A price is set by a public body rather than the market. It is not too strong perhaps to say that it approaches blasphemy. Even if the minimum wage has no ill effects or even if it had net positive effects (which, of course, most of these people claim is impossible),[36] it should not be allowed to stand. It is a glaring impurity, and that is reason enough to oppose it. Friedman himself listed it among the policies he would instantly repeal.[37]

Rob Norton, writing in *Fortune* in 1996, echoed this view. Even if the minimum wage did not have any adverse effects, it still raises a question:

> Before you sign on in favor of boosting the minimum wage, there's still a question that's hardly ever asked but should be: Is it fair? Specifically, is it fair to stick the employers of minimum-wage workers with the bill?
>
> To consider this question, you have to consider another: Why do employers pay some workers so little? The main reason—heartless though it may sound—is that that's all their work is worth. Please note that we're talking about the primary definition of the word "worth" ("material value, especially as expressed in terms of money") not the secondary one ("that quality of a person or thing that lends importance, value, merit, etc."). Failure to distinguish between the two has caused much of the general confusion about the minimum wage. . . .

Once you accept the fact that some work is not worth the minimum wage, you see the minimum-wage program for what it is: a not-so-well-focused public welfare program. This leads up to our final question: Why should the costs of the minimum wage be borne by the employers of minimum-wage workers?[38]

Or, consider James Bovard's position:

In 1930 a man could sell his labor to whomever he pleased, on almost any mutually acceptable terms. Now a person can no longer profit from the use of his hands or mind as he chooses, but must conform to hundreds of government decrees on "fair" labor. Since politicians first claimed the power to define fair labor standards, they have constantly expanded their control, continually creating new absurdities and new disruptions of voluntary private contracts. . . .

The FLSA [Fair Labor Standards Act, the federal minimum wage and maximum hours law] restricts opportunity and violates basic morality. Just as no man is entitled to a share of his neighbor's income, no man is entitled to have his neighbor's freedom restricted in order to boost his own income.[39]

In addition to the ideological offense the minimum wage gives to true believers, it has strong symbolic overtones, for it penetrates into one of the most basic of business decisions. Many free marketeers will grudgingly admit that governmental regulation in certain areas is justifiable, if kept modest. Many of them will confess that such a "collective goods" problem as pollution calls for some governmental oversight.[40] The minimum wage, however, reaches more directly into the firm than the normal regulatory directive does. As long as the minimum wage stands, a potentially far-reaching governmental economic trusteeship is therefore legitimated.

These two factors explain the visceral reaction any suggestion of a minimum wage increase provokes. Most of the time the policy's existence can be forgotten, like the blasphemer who remains silent; but when its banner is hoisted, it inflicts an emotional scar. All talk of impact, data, and so forth are therefore irrelevant.

Although the ideologues form a noisy vanguard, there are always some members of Congress who are reflexively opposed to the minimum wage but only sit in the middle pews of the free market church.

They generally prefer markets and doubt the wisdom of interfering in them without good reason. In the final analysis, however, they consider markets instruments, not a set of theological propositions. Thus, whether swayed by argumentation or political considerations, some of them usually end up supporting a minimum wage increase, as long as it is not too great.[41] This explains why minimum wage increases manage to pass at all and why they tend to be rather limited.

The opposing covey of members of Congress, their allies in such think tanks as the Economic Policy Institute, the Center for Budget and Policy Priorities, and to an extent the Brookings Institution, and their team of supportive academics and journalists are the heirs of New Deal liberalism. There were basically two facets of the New Deal: modest regulation of the macroeconomy to promote full employment and growth and mild redistributive policies to help those on the lower rungs of the economic ladder. When enacted, the minimum wage stood astride both these thrusts. Its designated aims were to increase purchasing power to help stave off deeper recessions and to fight poverty.

Modern liberals have turned to other techniques of demand stimulation to regulate the economy, when they have had the chance. No mention is ever made of the minimum wage in this context. It has instead become a social welfare policy.

Modern social welfare liberals are largely what Mickey Kaus has called "money liberals."[42] Their chief goal, in short, is to increase the incomes of the poor. The rationale for doing this is twofold. One is to move as many people as possible out of poverty. Ever since the Great Society's war on poverty, social welfare liberals have cited data on how many people are below the official poverty line as proof that "something must be done." The other is to reduce economic inequality. Modern social welfare liberals repeatedly state that economic inequality is, by almost any measure, greater in the United States than in any other advanced industrial democracy and that it has been growing over the last generation. They seldom, however, explain why this is undesirable or why government should do anything about it. One supposes that it is self-evident, steep comparative inequality being bad as a given.

The favored tool of social welfare liberals to increase the actual incomes of the poor is a cash transfer of some type. Cash transfers, they argue, have two advantages over other policy options, such as the direct provision of services. First, they give the poor choices. They are free to allocate their resources as they see fit, not in the manner a paternalistic state would if it provided direct services or stipulated how money was to be spent. Resources give the poor access to the good things of life, and they can choose what mix of goods they desire. Second, it is the most economically efficient way to bring people up to a certain standard or to reduce inequality. Government can collect money from some people and transfer it to others much more efficiently—that is, at less cost per dollar transferred—than it can create bureaucratic institutions to carry out programs. Spending can be targeted where it will accomplish the most good, with a minimum of administrative cost.

The net result is that the minimum wage has become something of a policy stepchild to social welfare liberals, in the family but not sharing the gene pool. It is, after all, not a very efficient way to transfer money to the poor. Many of those who get some of the raise, about a third as we see later, are teenagers, most of whom are not supporting families. It therefore fails both the targeting and economic efficiency tests. At the same time, it is not under the direct control of government, which gives it a certain invisibility.

Take the most thoroughgoing intellectual defense of the welfare state, written by Norman Furniss and Timothy Tilton in 1977. They offered a lengthy list of proposed reforms to strengthen the welfare state, including a guaranteed annual income, which would "operate much like a negative income tax, save that it will go to every citizen by right."[43] A minimum wage is not even mentioned in their wish list. Almost a decade later, B. Guy Peters, a warm partisan of the welfare state, wrote of its "crisis." He, too, neglected to mention the minimum wage in his survey of various policies, concentrating entirely on policies entailing direct spending.[44]

This tendency to consider the minimum wage a marginal add-on to more central welfare state policies shows up in the liberal journals of opinion when minimum wage increases are being discussed in Congress. In the midst of the 1996 battle over a minimum wage hike, the editors of the *Progressive* published a "Comment" entitled "Greed

Lives."[45] It began by attacking the *Wall Street Journal*'s purported concern for low-wage workers. That point was followed by a suggestion that the minimum wage should at least catch up with the inflation that had occurred since its last increase. "We need," the writer next argued, "a more comprehensive approach to the growing problem of poverty in the United States. Even as the minimum wage debate inches forward, we are rapidly moving backward on other fronts." The author then moved into a six-paragraph diatribe against cutting Aid to Families with Dependent Children (AFDC). Those words obviously burned with more passion than the need for a minimum wage hike.

About the same time, Barry Bluestone and Teresa Ghilarducci wrote an article for the *American Prospect* entitled "Rewarding Work: A Feasible Antipoverty Policy."[46] They first cited the usual dreary statistics on poverty in the United States. Then they pointed to four advantages of the minimum wage: (1) it imposes no burden on taxpayers, (2) it raises the incomes of many people who do not receive transfer payments, (3) it provides an incentive to work, and (4) it can lead to greater productivity. The second half of the article turned to an analysis of the Earned Income Tax Credit. The central point was that these two policies complement each other as antipoverty tools. That the minimum wage is a work incentive and can effect greater productivity consequently got shoved completely aside.

In short, social welfare liberals view the minimum wage primarily as a cash transfer program, and a not very important one at that. If it moves onto the active political agenda, they will swing behind it, both for its marginal contribution to fighting poverty and for its symbolic value. It is a symbol of society's continuing commitment to the poor and therefore worth a skirmish. But it does not stir the passions as it does for the opponents or as other policies do for social welfare liberals.

The symbolic nature of minimum wage politics from the pro side is further underscored by looking at the groups that join in lobbying for an increase. Civil rights and women's organizations can be found advocating an increase any time it begins to get serious political attention. This is true even of sections of the African American community and women's movement that one would not ordinarily expect to stand with minimum wage proponents. For example, the magazine *Black En-*

terprise, which caters to black business owners, carried an article by Edward Irons in its December 1995 issue strongly supporting an increase in the minimum wage. After decrying the nation's growing inequality, he said, "The best response to this scenario is to raise the minimum wage of full-time wage earners above the poverty level and to index the increase to protect purchasing power."[47] Likewise, the executive director of the Business and Professional Women's Association testified at congressional hearings in favor of a minimum wage increase.[48] Even though most of its members are employers, she stressed, the association identified with women who make the minimum wage.

The political heavy hitters in the pro–minimum wage camp are unions. Whenever a minimum wage increase is under consideration, they can be counted on to devote substantial energy to the cause. This represents an interesting transformation, since the American Federation of Labor opposed the early state minimum wage laws and labor as a whole was lukewarm to the Fair Labor Standards Act in 1938, the law that established the federal minimum wage. Since the late 1940s, though, when labor and Harry Truman became close allies, labor has stood firmly for minimum wage increases. This support, too, must be counted as largely marshaled for symbolic purposes, though. Few union members make the minimum wage, and, while a few union contracts, particularly in the clothing industry, have sometimes called for wages to be set at multiples of the minimum wage, there is little evidence that the "ripple effect" of a minimum wage increase reaches many unionized workers. Nevertheless, it is a policy that symbolizes the political system's commitment to working people. It calls for a graphic yes-no vote on a wage increase for people who are working. Unions thus feel it is important enough to justify committing substantial resources on its behalf.

The Political Economy of Citizenship

The political philosopher Michael Sandel has noted:

In contemporary American politics, most of our economic arguments revolve around two considerations: prosperity and fairness. . . .

So familiar are these ways of justifying economic policy that they might seem to exhaust the possibilities. But our debates about economic policy have not always focused solely on the size and distribution of the national product. Throughout much of American history they have also addressed a different question, namely what economic arrangements are most hospitable to self government? Along with prosperity and fairness, the civic consequences of economic policy have often loomed large in American political discourse.[49]

Taking up the civic consequences of economic policy would lead us to what Sandel calls the political economy of citizenship. Such a political economy is based on the civic republican tradition, not the individualist ideas of democracy that have held sway in American life since at least the early 1960s. Individualist democracy is in some ways the political analogue of market economics. It glorifies individual choice without passing judgment on what the nature of those choices are. It therefore leads to a view of liberty that involves the assertion of rights as claims that society must respect. The political process is just if it is procedurally fair—if, that is, it aggregates individual preferences accurately, in the same way a properly functioning market aggregates consumer choices.

Civic republicanism, in contrast, places people within community and takes the view that liberty lies in participating in the life of that community.[50] The identity of citizen is a part of what gives definition to life. Given this communal focus, it is not surprising civic republicans believe there is a public interest that is separate and distinct from the mere summing up of every individual's preferences. Politics, therefore, should be devoted to the task of searching out and trying to reach the public interest. Republics also rest on the virtue of the citizenry, not self-interest, no matter how defined. Thus, it is perfectly legitimate, in fact imperative, that the government take an active role in developing virtue in the citizenry. Obviously, much of that virtue will be taught while citizens are in their formative years; however, encouraging virtue continues throughout life.

What would a politics of the minimum wage informed by the political economy of citizenship look like? Although there are any number of ramifications, three major issues stand out immediately. There is, first of all, the social value of work. Traditional economic theory assigns work a purely negative value. One works to obtain money; hence, the less work one can do for the money the better. But modern social scientists are rediscovering the fact that work has quite a few more faces than this. A variety of social and psychological aspects of work are as important as its economic qualities, and many of these are closely tied to issues surrounding citizenship. A political economy of citizenship would therefore ask, for example, which of the features of work contribute to and which detract from citizenship. Is work a prerequisite for citizenship? Should any cash transfers be made without work? To what extent should there be a political commitment to provide work, or meaningful work, for all who wish it? If we expect every adult to work, should we not make that work carry a remuneration commensurate with the requirements of citizenship?

Second, there is the question of whether a relationship exists between having an economic stake in the community and citizenship. Many political thinkers in the late eighteenth and early nineteenth centuries argued that political participation should be restricted to those who possessed a certain amount of property. Being a property owner, it was thought, induced sobriety of character, provided an indelible psychological link with the fate of the community, and married one's own economic interest to that of the community. Although confining political participation in such a fashion is obviously untenable today, this rationale may bear reexamining and the question turned around. Presuming universal citizenship, if having an economic stake in the community helps cultivate better citizens, should everyone be encouraged to acquire such a stake? If so, to what degree should public policy be employed to secure this end?

Third, there is the vitally important issue of how economic inequality affects the bonds of common citizenship and basic political equality. When does either opulent luxury or debilitating poverty erode the character traits necessary for healthy citizenship? Do sharp economic inequalities undermine the public institutions—public schools, parks, transportation facilities, the military—that build common ties in a community? How great can economic disparities become before there is such a psychological distance between people of different income groups that they cannot feel a common identity or perceive their lives as bound together in a common destiny?

A political economy of citizenship regarding the minimum wage would therefore witness a debate over the value of work, the need for citizens to have a stake in the community, and the effects of economic inequality on political equality, themes that are taken up again in the concluding chapter.

Eldon Eisenach has argued that the legal realists of the 1920s claimed the mantle of intellectual descendants of the Progressives. But their positivism in methodology, he notes, led to relativistic substantive conclusions, thereby detaching Progressive thinking from its religious moorings and making it empty in the end. Modern social welfare liberals do something of the same thing in the economic realm. Partisans of "fairness," they view the political system as an apparatus for making cash transfers in an economically efficient fashion, but they have strayed far from the basic value assumptions of why that is wise public policy. In so doing, they have entered the church of the free marketeers, even if they sit in the back pews, seldom put much in the offering plate, and often leave before the final hymn. They have accepted individual consumer sovereignty as a good and employed economic efficiency as a central criterion for policy success. This puts them squarely within a neoclassical economic framework.[51]

Eisenach also contends that Wilsonian interest group politics was mostly responsible for destroying Progressivism as a political movement. Although it is debatable how much the Wilson administration was to blame for the development of interest group politics among those who favored Progressive public policies, it does not seem debatable that modern social welfare liberals often think of interest group pluralism as the path to governing. Talk of "rainbow coalitions" and an assortment of other euphemisms belies this position, as does the recitation of who will get how much when minimum wage increases are discussed.[52] This type of interest group politics utterly fails to address people as citizens searching for a common good. Eisenach emphasizes that we can unearth the lost promise of Progressivism only by turning again to civic republicanism. If we do so, it would induce a serious rethinking of the minimum wage.

2

A Brief Political History through 1989

Soon after Massachusetts passed the first American minimum wage law, a number of other states adopted similar statutes. By the end of World War I, minimum wage laws were spreading further through the states, even if they were restricted in scope and anemic in their enforcement. Then, in 1923, the Supreme Court struck down the minimum wage law for the District of Columbia, and the political tide turned. Where the laws were not repealed, they fell rapidly into disuse.

The onset of the Great Depression revived the movement for minimum wages, leading several states to respond with new statutes. At the federal level, the National Industrial Recovery Act of 1933, the first major initiative of the Roosevelt administration aimed at alleviating the depression, contained a minimum wage provision. The Supreme Court struck this measure down, however, and the idea languished until 1937.

Congress established the current federal minimum wage program in the Fair Labor Standards Act of 1938 (FLSA), the last major domestic reform of the New Deal. Although the act contained a maximum hours provision and a ban on child labor, it was always intended primarily as a minimum wage statute. When it passed, Franklin D. Roosevelt declared that, except for social security, it was "the most far-reaching, far-sighted program for the benefit of the workers ever adopted here or in any other country."[1] It was not amended until eleven years later, but periodically ever since it has been the subject of intense political controversy.

Early State Minimum Wage Laws

Massachusetts's law of 1912 applied only to women and minors working in certain industries.[2] Moreover, it was riddled with exceptions, such as exclusions for apprentices and handicapped workers. Administratively, it followed the Australian precedent and created a separate wage board for each covered industry. These boards, composed of representatives of employers, employees, and "the public," were to set the wage, using loose guidelines laid out in the law. The chief one decreed that the wage should be adequate "to supply the necessary cost of living and to maintain the worker in health."[3] The only sanction against firms paying less than the minimum, though, was publicity. The names of offenders were handed over to a body known as the Minimum Wage Commission, which was responsible for publishing the names in all the newspapers of the state.

The following year eight states—Oregon, Utah, Washington, Nebraska, Minnesota, Colorado, California, and Wisconsin—adopted similar laws. Kansas and Arkansas followed suit in 1915, as did Arizona in 1917. In 1919, North Dakota and Texas joined the fold, followed by South Dakota in 1923. Meanwhile, in 1918, Congress passed a similar measure for the District of Columbia. All of these statutes restricted the coverage to women or to women and minors. Most followed the Massachusetts prototype, forming a series of wage boards. As for enforcement, only Nebraska copied the publicity alone strategy; the others instituted a variety of fines and prison terms for violators. Some also included a provision whereby an underpaid employee could bring a civil suit for recovery of back wages.

The 1920s were not kind to minimum wage laws. Business interests succeeded in getting several states to repeal their statutes, while in others the enforcement mechanisms were emasculated. But the most important victories for minimum wage opponents came in the courts. In 1923, the Supreme Court voided the District of Columbia law on the grounds that it violated both the employer's and employee's "liberty of contract."[4] It took from the employer, the Court said, "an arbitrary payment for a purpose and upon a basis having no causal connection with his business." In the wake of this case, other state laws were struck down by the federal courts. By 1930, only seven state statutes were still standing, and few of them were being enforced with any regularity.

The onset of the Great Depression spurred renewed state activity. Seven states adopted minimum wage laws in 1933, and by 1938, twenty-five states had a statute on the books. Oklahoma ventured onto new territory by extending its law to men. Adopting a more flexible view of a state's "police powers" under the Constitution, the Supreme Court upheld Washington's minimum wage law in 1937,[5] and pending judicial challenges to the others faded away.

The National Industrial Recovery Act and Its Aftermath

Although Teddy Roosevelt's Progressive party's platform of 1912 called for the enactment of a national minimum wage, Congress did not seriously take up the idea until the advent of the New Deal.[6] Most of FDR's advisers felt that the root cause of the depression was the precipitate decline in purchasing power that had occurred since the stock market crash of 1929.[7] If purchasing power could be restored, business would recover, and employment would return to normal levels. Not yet ready to embrace a Keynesian surge in government spending, they sought ways to resurrect purchasing power through the private sector.

Their solution was the far-reaching National Industrial Recovery Act (NIRA).[8] Its core provisions empowered trade associations to draft codes of "fair competition" for their industries. The president would then approve the codes, giving them the force of law. A section of the "blanket code" that was to be included in each of the industrial codes called for the payment of minimum wages. The minimum wage was set at thirty cents per hour but with a "target wage" of forty cents. Privately, the president expressed the hope that most industries would move their minimums even higher.

The minimum wage proved to be the most popular part of the NIRA. Many letters from ordinary workers to the National Recovery Administration (NRA), the administrative arm of the NIRA, remain poignant reminders of peoples' feelings:[9]

> The fair employer is certainly for the NRA. The NRA places a minimum wage, so the man paying $13 a week don't have to compete with one paying $3 a week. Those who don't like the NRA never have worked in a sweatshop.
>
> If the poor people could only express themselves like the rich there would

be no question as to whether NRA had been a benefit to the working classes or not.

Our life is no bed of roses because that ain't the way it is for workers yet but it's better for us than ever I seen it and I been in a factory 9 years since I was 15.

[The minimum wage makes] a big difference and our life is different and there is a chance for a happy home.

Nevertheless, the Supreme Court struck down the NIRA in 1935, saying that it unconstitutionally delegated legislative power to the executive branch.[10] Unfortunately for the administration and American workers, it was a conclusion with which most legal scholars agreed.

Even though the Court had stymied the federal government's initial foray into setting wages, the economic arguments that had driven the NIRA remained convincing to many in Roosevelt's inner circle. The administration was moving slowly to the political left, and the 1936 Democratic platform included an unambiguous plank calling for a general minimum wage. Soon after his crushing victory in the election, Roosevelt announced, "The people, by overwhelming vote, are in favor of a floor below which wages shall not fall."[11]

Even if Roosevelt had been able to secure favorable action in Congress, however, the Supreme Court remained a barrier to the extension of federal economic power.[12] Soon, however, a case involving labor relations paved the way for a national minimum wage. The Wagner Act of 1935 had provided protections to unions seeking collective bargaining agreements. Congress claimed that the authority to enact the statute lay in the commerce clause of the Constitution, which grants Congress the power "to regulate commerce . . . among the several states." Since 1890, the Supreme Court had been construing the reach of federal power under this clause quite narrowly, separating commerce from production. If this line of thinking remained dominant, the Wagner Act was as doomed as the NIRA. However, the Court reversed course and upheld the law.[13] The door had finally swung open for Congress to move into other areas of economic life with little fear of judicial obstruction.

Passage of the Fair Labor Standards Act of 1938

With that ruling, Roosevelt renewed his push for a minimum wage and maximum hours law. His message to Congress accompanying the administration's bill contained his famous observation that "one third of our population . . . is ill-nourished, ill-clad, and ill-housed."[14] A national minimum wage, the president contended, would accomplish three objectives: (1) protect workers from competition, (2) halt the downward spiral of wages, and (3) increase purchasing power.

The administration's bill set a base minimum wage of forty cents per hour. At the same time, it created the Labor Standards Board, which could set wages above this level in specific industries or occupations. The act was to apply to all those engaged in manufacturing, mining, transportation, and public utilities if the products or services they handled moved in interstate commerce. Professionals, executives, and supervisors were excluded from the act's reach; all workers in the agricultural and retail sectors were also exempt.[15] Moreover, the Labor Standards Board was handed the authority to grant further exemptions for "small employers" and apprentices. Enforcement of the act was to come from a ban on interstate shipments of any product manufactured or transported in violation of the law.

Only a handful of presidential proposals have stirred more controversy. Opponents called it a "tyrannical industrial dictatorship" that would hand business over "to the mercies of [a] multiplying and hampering Federal bureaucracy."[16] Many observers gave it little chance of passage.

When the Senate Labor Committee finally finished its work on the bill, significant changes had been introduced. First, the power of the Labor Standards Board had been reversed; it now only had the power to set specific industrial or occupational wages *below* the statutory minimum. Moreover, the board was allowed to establish regional differentials, something southern business interests strongly desired. Further, the new proposal mandated that the board had to utilize industry advisory committees when considering the wage levels for various industries. This was an attempt to insert business political clout directly into administrative decision making. On the Senate floor, numerous amendments were submitted, and several succeeded. The more important of these broadened the agricultural exemption somewhat and added a number of criteria to be considered by the Labor Standards Board, such as transportation costs and "local economic conditions" (another gesture to southerners). The severely amended, watered-down version then passed the Senate by a lopsided two-to-one margin. The bill's opponents were satisfied that they had largely obtunded the measure, but proponents did not deign to vote against it.

Meanwhile, the House Labor Committee was modifying the bill along other lines. It inserted a provision outlawing gender discrimination, set geographic requirements for membership on the Labor Standards Board, and added a stipulation that the board could act only in cases where collective bargaining was ineffective.[17]

According to the procedures of the House of Representatives, bills approved by its standing committees must go to the Rules Committee to secure a place on the floor calendar. Technically, this committee was designed to act as a "traffic cop," merely ensuring the smooth flow of business. However, during this period, it often used its scheduling powers to block legislation it opposed. Controlled by senior conservative Democrats from the South, the committee bottled up the minimum wage bill. It languished there until Congress adjourned, seemingly dead.

FDR responded by calling a special session of Congress and making the Fair Labor Standards Act a top priority. The Senate fairly quickly readopted its bill from the previous session. The House Labor Committee, however, changed its bill to provide for a flat national minimum wage and the vesting of administrative authority in a single agency rather than a board. The Rules Committee again refused to place it on the calendar. Supporters began a discharge petition, a procedure that can pry a bill out of a House committee if 218 signatures are obtained. The effort stalled, though.

Fate intervened in the form of a Democratic primary for a Florida Senate seat. Claude Pepper won a major victory in this election, using the Fair Labor Standards Act as his main campaign theme. Within two and a half hours after the House convened the next day, the discharge petition secured the necessary signatures.

An intense and emotional floor debate followed. The bill finally passed, setting a minimum wage of twenty-five cents per hour, with increases of five cents per year until it reached forty cents. The agricultural and retail exemptions were broadened even further, but no differentials were to be allowed.

The conference committee managed to piece together a generally acceptable compromise. The wage was kept at twenty-five cents, but a series of steps was to increase it to forty cents by 1945. The agricultural and retail exemptions remained quite broad, but no legal differentials were created. Administration and enforcement were handed over to the newly created Wage and Hour Division. Industry committees were to be set up under its aegis that could recommend higher minimums to the head of the division, who could then implement them if he chose. Enforcement was strengthened by authorizing both the Wage and Hour Division and individual workers (or their "agents," i.e., unions) to bring civil suits for back wages, along with the ban on interstate shipment of goods made or transported by workers not paid the minimum wage.

The basic structure of the Fair Labor Standards Act has remained intact, a national minimum for all covered workers. Subsequent political controversies have revolved primarily around the level of the wage and who is to be covered by the act.[18]

The Mixed Bag of 1949

President Truman suggested raising the minimum wage during the 1948 presidential campaign and repeated the recommendation in the eight-point program of reform laid out in his 1949 State of the Union message. Three weeks later, the administration sent Congress a bill, raising the wage level to seventy-five cents and expanding coverage to all those whose work was "affected" by interstate commerce, an estimated five million people. The measure was, administration spokesmen said, "just another insurance policy for this country against any depression."[19]

Congressional Republicans, however, were in no mood to co-operate with the administration. Relations had been strained severely by the bruising battle over the Taft-Hartley Act in 1948. Furthermore, many GOP lawmakers wanted to strike back at the now heavily Democratic federal judiciary. A series of decisions by the courts of appeals that had stretched the meaning of the coverage provisions of the FLSA seemed to provide an easy target for retribution.[20] In further sniping, Congress had passed the Portal-to-Portal Act over Truman's veto, a measure that cut back on some of the FLSA's maximum hours sections.

Believing that an increase would have negligible economic effects given the postwar inflation, opponents concentrated their fire on the act's coverage. They also tried to get the minimum wage tied to the cost of living, an especially interesting move considering later developments. At the time, fear of rapid price declines was as alive as fear of inflation. Dominated by moderates, the labor committees of both houses reported out bills raising the minimum wage by thirty-five cents and slightly increasing coverage. Once again, though, the House Rules Committee sat on the bill.

A group of conservative Republicans and southern Democrats cobbled together a "compromise" that raised the wage level to seventy-five cents but actually cut back on the act's core coverage. They proposed to make only those whose work was "indispensable" to interstate commerce subject to the act rather than those whose jobs were "closely related . . . or necessary to" it, as the 1938 statute provided. Truman's allies fought to stave off this attack on the reach of the act but were only moderately successful. They managed to have "directly essential" rather than "indispensable" put in the definition, but even this was a good bit more restrictive. Furthermore, they had to acquiesce in making the retail exemption even broader to obtain this concession.

Truman viewed the measure as a bitter setback, but he could not bring himself to veto it. The administration thus won its battle for a higher minimum, but it was a Pyrrhic victory. The Department of Labor estimated that while approximately 1.5 million people would receive a raise, around 1.0 million other workers would permanently lose the protection of the act.[21]

The lesson of this session was that the minimum wage was not on any automatic and inevitable march toward higher wages and expanded coverage. Political conditions at any given session of Congress could lead to setbacks just as well as gains in either area, even though outright repeal of the statute appeared unlikely (see figures 2 and 3 for increases in the minimum wage over the years).

The Eisenhower Administration

Eisenhower's first two years as president were accompanied by a Republican majority in both houses of Congress, resulting in little sympathy for movement on the minimum wage front. When the Democrats regained control of Congress in 1954, however, the administration sought policies that lay on common ground. In December of 1954, Secretary of Labor James Mitchell, who had expressed public dismay at the modest coverage of the minimum wage, urged the president to recommend a boost to eighty-five or ninety cents an hour and coverage for retail workers.[22] Eisenhower took the advice and included both suggestions in his 1955 State of the Union address.

Senate liberals began pushing for $1.25, but Mitchell raised fears of inflation if they exceeded the $.90 target. In the end, both the House

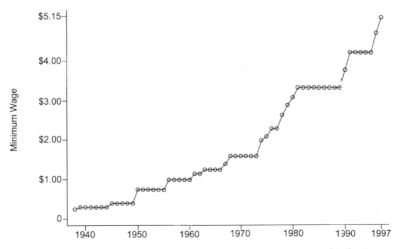

Figure 2. Increases in the Minimum Wage (*Source:* Department of Labor)

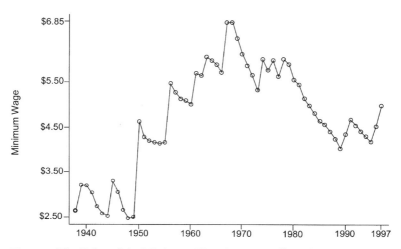

Figure 3. The Value of the Minimum Wage in 1995 Dollars (*Source:* Department of Labor and calculations by the author)

and Senate passed bills with a raise to $1.00 but postponed any consideration of new coverage. Mitchell said he was disappointed that coverage was not broadened, but he recommended that Eisenhower sign the bill, which he did.

In the waning days of the Eisenhower presidency, a more pitched battle over the minimum wage erupted. The president had halfheartedly recommended the coverage of retail workers every year after 1955, but the issue lay dormant until 1959. Senator John F. Kennedy introduced a bill that year to cover retail workers and raise the wage to $1.25. He managed to steer the measure through the Labor and Public Welfare Committee and onto the floor. In the end, the Senate gave its approval to a slightly revised version, exempting small retailers and restaurants, hotels, and motels from the new provisions.

In the House, the liberal-dominated Education and Labor Committee set a $1.25 minimum wage but adopted a novel approach to coverage. Instead of listing categories of enterprises, it simply said that all retail firms annually grossing more than $1 million were subject to the act. This was an important departure because in all previous congressional enactments under the commerce clause, some particu-

lar product or activity had to touch interstate commerce. The rationale for the new approach was that under modern economic conditions, any retail business with $1 million in sales could hardly avoid
having out-of-state suppliers. With this new step, congressional regulation would become virtually unlimited. The committee bill thus en-
countered intense opposition on the floor. Moderates again moved to
craft a compromise, this time raising the wage to only $1.15 and add-
ing a sprinkling of new workers. It was this version that secured House
approval but only by an eight-vote margin.

By the time the conference committee took up the bill in the summer of 1960, Kennedy was the front-runner for the Democratic presidential nomination, and he asked to lead the Senate conferees. He signaled House moderates several times that he was ready to yield on the
wage level but not on coverage. Many of Kennedy's supporters urged
him to get what he could in the way of expanded coverage to gain the
higher wage, but he refused to budge. He promised throughout the
negotiations to make the minimum wage an issue in the fall campaign.

He followed through, on several occasions during stump speeches
castigating Republicans for blocking increased coverage. He even
mentioned it in the famous television debates with Richard Nixon.
After his election victory, Kennedy issued a list of his top five legislative priorities, prominent among which was an increased minimum
wage with expanded coverage.[23]

The Kennedy Administration's Victory of 1961

Early in 1961, Kennedy sent Congress a bill calling for a hike in the
minimum wage to $1.25 and, following the House Labor and Educa-
tion Committee's lead from the previous year, coverage for all those
working in retail enterprises with more than $1 million in sales. The
Department of Labor estimated that this would bring about 4.3 million new workers under the act.

The president's supporters in Congress had to fight off the salvos of
those who were disappointed by the timidity of the bill as well as the
usual chorus of minimum wage opponents. Labor leaders split openly
with the administration, one AFL-CIO official saying simply the bill

was "just not good enough."[24] Republicans and southern Democrats seemed pleased with the cleavage, because the minimum wage proposal was an early test of the political viability of Kennedy's whole New Frontier program.

The bill was sympathetically received in the Senate, where the final draft was a recognizable variant of the administration's proposals: a $1.25 wage level and the inclusion of the retail sales volume test with only minor adjustments. In the House, though, matters were not so easy. The Education and Labor Committee sent the administration bill to the floor, but the reception was chilly. Moderates mounted their usual "compromise" strategy. This time the package called for a scaled-back increase to $1.15 and inclusion of workers at only large retail chains. In the crucial vote, the more restricted coverage for retail workers won by a margin of one.

Because of the closeness of the House vote, Senate conferees decided that if they gave up a few specific categories of workers, they might be able to salvage the new retail definition. They proposed making the new test one of dollar volume but then exempting certain types of businesses from the test. They agreed to exempt all laundries, automobile and farm equipment dealerships, and cotton gins whatever their gross sales. This strategy worked, as a handful of House members changed over and voted to accept the conference report. Some senators carped about the omission of these unfortunate workers but believed they had no choice but to go along.

The minimum wage now stood at $1.25, and 3.6 million previously uncovered workers were brought under the act's umbrella. Further, the retail dollar volume test was in place. When the president signed the bill, he said with evident satisfaction that "we can move from this improvement into greater gains."[25]

The Great Society

Lyndon Johnson's huge victory in 1964 swept an unusually large Democratic majority into Congress, many of whom were strongly disposed to back the president's declaration of the War on Poverty and his blueprint for a Great Society. This favorable political climate for

Johnson's liberal programs both helped and hurt the prospects for new minimum wage legislation. On the plus side, both the administration and congressional leaders were inclined to increase the minimum wage and coverage. However, the centerpiece of the War on Poverty was a plethora of new federal spending programs, pushing the minimum wage to the fringe of the priority list. In essence, American social welfare liberalism was at high tide. Moreover, when the American commitment to Vietnam began to expand, many of Johnson's economic advisers feared a burst of inflation. A minimum wage boost, they told the president, could add to that problem.

Labor leaders, sensing the administration's movement to welfare expenditure policies, began pressing Johnson in early 1966 to devote political energy to hiking the wage level to $1.75 and stretching coverage. Johnson was reportedly wary of anything over $1.40 but did concur on the need to expand the scope of the act. The president belatedly announced a plan to raise the wage floor to $1.60 over two years and bring in an estimated 8.2 million additional workers. These new additions would come, first, from dropping the retail sales volume test to $250,000, while pulling in restaurants, hotels, and laundries. Second, employees of hospitals, nursing homes, schools, and colleges would be added to the rolls. Finally, agricultural workers employed on farms with seven or more full-time workers (about 1 percent of all agricultural workers) would gain protection. It was the first suggestion of penetrating the agricultural sector and was expected to be controversial.

The bill moved easily through the House Education and Labor Committee. On the floor, Republican leaders concentrated on raising the retail sales volume exemption and defeating the new coverage of agricultural workers. They failed on both scores, but by only five and eight votes, respectively. Opponents did manage, though, to have the new increase stretched out over three years, hoping inflation would thereby mitigate its impact.

The Senate passed the bill but modified it significantly. Elementary and secondary schools were removed from coverage, but a provision was inserted to require that any tipped employee had to be paid at least half the minimum wage. This latter modification had been eagerly sought by unions, since many firms with tipped employees counted all tips toward the minimum wage.[26] The new coverage of agricultural workers was retained, but the retail sales volume test was increased to $350,000.

In the conference committee, coverage was granted to workers in elementary and secondary schools, and the new tip provision was made part of the law. The retail sales volume test was put at the House-approved $250,000, but the new rate was to go into effect over three years rather than two.

The Confrontation of the Nixon Years

Although few of the major figures of the Nixon administration could be characterized as rabidly anti–minimum wage, their economic priorities lay elsewhere, chiefly in controlling inflation. Not unexpectedly, the administration did not initiate a push for new minimum wage legislation. Democratic leaders on the House Education and Labor Committee, however, introduced legislation in 1971 to increase the minimum wage to $2.00 and expand the law's application to a significant number of previously uncovered workers: domestic household workers; employees of the federal, state, and local governments; and a handful of additional agricultural workers.

On the floor, opponents, strongly backed by the Nixon administration, offered a substitute, granting the same raise to those already covered but containing no additions. Furthermore, it allowed employers to hire youths under eighteen or any full-time student at 80 percent of the minimum wage, triggering years of debate over a subminimum wage. Unions strongly opposed this idea, arguing that it would take jobs away from adults. The GOP substitute was the one that obtained House approval, though.

Senate Democrats settled on the House committee bill in the spring of 1972 but added a reduction in the retail dollar volume sales test to $150,000. Senate floor consideration came during the middle of the presidential campaign, giving all Democrats an added incentive to pass it. Accordingly, it emerged largely intact.

The conference committee's deliberations naturally became embroiled in election-year politics. The Democratic Speaker of the House tried to make the House delegation more liberal than the voting break-down on the bill's final passage would have normally justified. Thus, the House conferees would actually be more in accord with the Sen-ate version than with their own chamber's. When he refused to recon-sider his choices, irate Republicans combined with conservative Demo-crats to kill the bill by having the House refuse to go to conference at all. Democrats were not entirely displeased, because many thought it would be a good election year issue.

Early in 1973, both the House and Senate committees sent retreaded versions of their 1972 minimum wage bills to the floor. In an attempt to mollify the administration, the House included a scaled-down youth differential, allowing full-time students holding part-time jobs to be paid 85 percent of the minimum. The compromise glided through both houses. Nixon vetoed the measure, though, citing fears of inflation and arguing that what was needed was a blanket youth differential. A heated debate followed, but an attempt to override the veto fell 23 votes short in the House.

A year later, the president's political capital had fallen dramatically, and minimum wage advocates seized the opportunity. The Senate passed a bill raising the wage level to $2.20 and expanding coverage along the lines of its 1972 proposal. The House set the minimum wage at $2.30 but agreed to a pilot program of an 85 percent youth sub-minimum under certain highly restricted conditions. The conference committee opted for the $2.30 wage schedule and the youth subminimum. Presented with political realities, Nixon signed the bill this time.

The provision affecting state and local governments immediately became the subject of litigation. The Supreme Court first ruled that congressional power under the commerce clause could justify regula-tion of some state and local activities but not traditional governmen-tal functions.[27] After nine frustrating years of trying to define tradi-tional governmental functions, the Court overruled the case. State and local governments could adequately protect themselves, the justices said, through the normal political process.[28]

The Carter Years

Jimmy Carter's election in 1976 fueled the hopes of many Democratic constituencies, including advocates of a higher minimum wage. Two factors complicated any smooth passage of a new minimum wage law, however. First, Carter had run as an independent, purposely distancing himself from Washington leaders and traditional Democratic interest groups, such as unions. Second, the loosely organized civil rights lobby, having secured most of its legal goals, was turning its attention to economic issues, injecting yet another factor into the usual intricate and tangled bargaining processes surrounding minimum wage politics.

Carter was inclined to suggest a modest increase in the minimum wage, but labor leaders pressured him to push for a more broadly based reform. He ended up taking their lead, sending Congress a bill in July 1977 calling for an immediate hike to $2.65 and indexing future raises to half the average manufacturing wage, beginning in 1978.

The House Education and Labor Committee added a change in the tip credit but otherwise stuck to the administration's proposal. The committee recommended that the tip credit be changed to $1.00 per hour rather than 50 percent of the minimum wage, a change eagerly sought by unions. The indexing feature was ripped out of the bill on the House floor; instead, a raise to $3.05 was to be accomplished in three steps. Another defeat for the minimum wage coalition came when the House restored the 50 percent tip credit. Lawmakers also voted to increase the retail sales volume exemption to $500,000. The most blistering battle was waged over a renewed effort to have a general subminimum added to the law. Hardly any employers had taken advantage of the subminimum adopted in 1974, leading critics to argue that it should be made broader and simpler. On the key vote, Speaker Tip O'Neil had to break a tie, keeping the amendment out of the bill.

The Senate's newly christened Human Resources Committee was largely in step with its House counterpart, but the Senate floor was another matter. The indexing provision was defeated there also, with the amount set at $3.40 in four steps. Faring better, the tip credit was set at 30 percent, while several versions of the youth subminimum were defeated. The retail sales volume exemption was increased to $325,000.

At the conference, the halfway game was played this time. A four-step adjustment to $3.35 was made in the wage level; the tip credit was made 40 percent; and the retail exemption was raised to $362,500.

The Reagan-Bush Years

Ronald Reagan steadfastly opposed any increase in the minimum wage. He made his position clear during the 1980 campaign when he said, "The minimum wage has caused more misery and unemployment than anything since the Great Depression," and again in 1983 when he told an audience, "A lot of our ills are due to the minimum wage."[29] As a result, the only initiative his administration took was to revive the idea of a youth subminimum in 1985, but nothing came of it. Minimum wage advocates pushed for an increase in 1987 but could not muster the votes to pass it.

Soon after George Bush was inaugurated, he signaled a willingness to approve an increase in the wage floor to $4.25 as a part of his bid for a "kinder, gentler" brand of conservative Republicanism. However, he coupled this offer with a demand that a youth subminimum "training wage" lasting six months be instituted for any newly hired worker.

Congressional Democrats thought they had strong public support for an even larger increase, given what the poll numbers were showing. Moreover, since Bush was simultaneously pushing for a capital gains tax cut, the bulk of which would go to the more affluent, they believed they could either force him to sign on to a higher figure or put him in an intolerable political position if he took out his veto pen. As before, labor leaders were adamant in their opposition to the subminimum.

While testifying before the Senate's Labor and Human Resources Committee, Secretary of Labor Elizabeth Dole insisted that any bill going over $4.25 would trigger a veto. Democrats brushed the threat aside and drafted a bill raising the wage to $4.65 with no training wage. They did go back to 50 percent for the tip credit, though, and changed the structure of the small business exemption. Until then, the exemption had applied only to retail and service firms. The new provision would extend the exemption to all businesses and set the amount at $500,000. On the floor, the increase was pushed back to $4.55, and a two-month training wage at 85 percent of the minimum was to be allowed for all employees. During the Senate debate, the administration repeated its veto threat almost daily.

Over in the House, the Education and Labor Committee's draft generally followed the Senate bill. The chief departure was the creation of a minimum wage review board, which would issue annual reports to Congress suggesting when and by how much the minimum wage should be increased. On the floor, the $4.55 level and the two-month, 85 percent training wage were both adopted, along with the higher tip credit and unified small business exemption. Despite charges that the review board was merely a backdoor way to index the minimum wage, it remained in the bill.

As the conference committee began work, Bush personally vowed that he would veto anything over $4.25. Congressional leaders thought he was bluffing and stuck to $4.55. With both houses set to concur on the report, a coalition of unions, civil rights groups, and women's organizations launched a nationwide radio advertising and letter-writing campaign urging the president not to veto the act. Underlining what political commentators saw as a new "get tough" approach, Bush vetoed the bill a mere fifty-five minutes after its passage, while aloft in Air Force One. The following day, a veto override attempt in the House fell 37 votes short.

Democratic leaders soon discovered that their political strategy had failed. There was little public outcry over the veto, leaving Bush unscathed. Nonetheless, Republican moderates worried openly that if the minimum wage issue surfaced again, the party could suffer serious political fallout. A short time later, a visit by Polish labor leader and future president Lech Wałęsa served to bring the two sides face-to-face. At a meeting between union leaders and White House personnel to plan details for the visit, negotiations began on a compromise minimum wage bill with which both sides could live.

While Democrats with strong labor ties and staunchly conservative Republicans shunned talk of a compromise, more flexible lawmakers on both sides began seeking common ground. Since Bush had stressed the $4.25 figure, it was hard for the White House to agree to anything more. Further, the aftermath of the veto had made many House Democrats feel they had to consent to some type of subminimum wage to avoid a replay. At the same time, uneasy Republicans were telling Bush that if a compromise contained the $4.25 figure, the arcane details of the training wage would be lost on the public and that he would be damaged by another veto.

The House managed to pass a patched-together bill holding to the $4.25 ceiling and establishing a three-month training wage limited to teenagers. Bush had wanted a training wage for any new hire, regardless of age or past work experience. Moreover, Democrats won a point by having the training wage expire in 1993, when they hoped a Democrat would be in the White House. Without much controversy, a general small business exemption was established for firms with less than

Table 1. Major Changes in the Minimum Wage Law

Year	Major Changes
1949	Reduced coverage by redefining meaning of *production* for interstate commerce.
	Reduced coverage by expanding the retail exemption.
1961	Coverage expanded by creation of an "enterprise test" for retail firms. All retail businesses with sales over $1 million now covered.
1966	Added hospitals, nursing homes, and schools and colleges to ranks of covered enterprises.
	Added laundries, restaurants, and hotels to list of covered enterprises (subject to sales volume test).
	Reduced retail sales volume test to $250,000.
	Extended coverage to certain agricultural workers.
	Tip credit set at 50 percent of the minimum wage.
1974	Coverage extended to domestic workers and employees of state and local governments.
	Subminimum wage of 85 percent of minimum wage allowed for full-time students under certain conditions.
1977	Tip credit reduced to 40 percent.
	Retail dollar volume test raised to $362,500.
1989	Three-month subminimum "training wage" allowed for teenagers.
	Retail dollar volume test raised to $500,000.

$500,000 in gross sales. (However, a technical change in the wording of another section of the statute soon canceled out the effect of this move, the details of which are provided in chapter 5.) Because a number of senators had been in on the bargaining process, the bill glided to passage there also, and Bush hurriedly signed it. Few of the politicians involved were happy with the outcome, but minimum wage workers could look forward to an increase in their paychecks for the first time since 1981 (see table 1 for major changes in the minimum wage law from 1949 to 1989).

The minimum wage was to be raised again in 1996, a story that is told in chapter 5.

3
Public Opinion

Without question, the American public is supportive of the federal minimum wage program. When the original bill was being considered in the 1930s, substantial majorities reported to pollsters that they favored passage of the Fair Labor Standards Act. In subsequent years, there has always been solid support for raising the minimum wage, usually hovering around three-fourths of the public. While a majority in every demographic group agrees that the national wage floor should be higher, there are differences among various segments of the population.

Despite this nearly universal backing for a higher minimum wage, the matter is not particularly salient. When asked the most important problem people want politicians to address, they seldom mention the minimum wage. Nonetheless, when presented with a question asking whether a candidate's stand on the minimum wage is important, many people answer in the affirmative, although after elections, few report that the minimum wage actually influenced their vote. When given a list of accomplishments of a particular administration, however, raising the minimum wage ranks near the middle.

Somewhat surprisingly, the public is fairly knowledgeable about the policy, even though only a small percentage of American workers are directly affected by it. Furthermore, most believe the program is beneficial to the economy in general and to various groups of workers in particular. In addition, they are quite skeptical about the negative effects of the minimum wage that economists most often claim.

Perhaps most interesting is that a sense of concern for one's fellow citizens flows through the public opinion data. Not only do three-fourths of the people favor raising the wages of at most 8 percent of the work force, they also usually favor setting the wage level higher than whatever Congress is considering at the moment. Moreover, when asked to face costs to themselves in the form of higher prices or taxes, the public still wishes to see the minimum wage hiked. Evidently, civic consciousness remains a feature of the American ethos.

Support for the Program

The Roosevelt administration enjoyed broad public support for its minimum wage proposals from the beginning. In 1936, while the president was entangled in a battle with the Supreme Court over the constitutionality of a number of New Deal initiatives, 70 percent of Americans said they favored a constitutional amendment "to regulate minimum wages."[1] Two polls conducted the following year showed continued support for the program. When asked whether "the Federal Government ought to set the lowest wage that employees should receive in each business and industry," 61 percent responded affirmatively.[2] When the question was worded more directly later in the year, inquiring whether one favored or opposed "a federal law providing for minimum wages and maximum hours," 69 percent were favorable.[3] In February 1938, as Roosevelt pressured Congress to enact the Fair Labor Standards Act, 67 percent supported the idea of a minimum wage law,[4] and in April, 59 percent said Congress should "pass a bill regulating wages and hours before ending this session."[5] In December, after the act was finally passed, people were asked if they favored "the new wage and hours law," and 71 percent declared they did.[6]

Since the adoption of the minimum wage law, the American public not only has continued to back the general concept but also has almost always favored a hike in the level of the wage. In all except one of the polls since 1945 that have asked this question, the public has stood solidly behind raising the minimum wage (see table 2). Especially since the 1970s, the percentage favoring an increase has hovered around 75–80 percent, remarkable support for a policy that affects only a small fraction of the people. Moreover, when asked whether they "strongly support" or "somewhat support" an increase, Americans opt for the former (see table 3).

While every demographic cohort advocates upping the minimum wage, there are notable distinctions among them. Since the general

Table 2. Support for Raising the Minimum Wage

Date of Poll	Percentage	Date of Poll	Percentage
1945	56	1988	76
1946	65	1989	84
1946	66	1989	87
1947	71	1993	64
1948	66	1994	73
1949	68	1994	75
1949	78	1995	72
1952	36	1995	78
1953	60	1995	78
1961	76	1995	78
1965	53	1995	79
1965	55	1996	85
1966	66	1996	84
1979	82	1996	78
1981	76	1996	78
1987	77	1996	78
1987	71	1996	80
1987	76	1996	77
1987	84	1996	89
1987	83		

Source: Compiled by the author.
Note: Some of the differences, especially in the same year, can probably be accounted for by differences in the wording of the question.

Table 3. Intensity of Public's Desire to Raise the Minimum Wage

Year	Strongly Support an Increase	Somewhat Support an Increase	Somewhat Oppose an Increase	Strongly Oppose an Increase
1987	59%	24%	7%	7%
1996	57	20	10	9
1996	60	20	8	8

Sources: Service Employees International Union Poll, May 25, 1987; NBC News/ *Wall Street Journal* Poll, May 15, 1996; NBC News/*Wall Street Journal* Poll, June 27, 1996.
Note: "Not sure" responses omitted.

pattern of responses has remained largely stable through time, one poll can be taken as indicative. The most recent is a *Time*/CNN poll taken in May of 1996 (see table 4).

Females favor increasing the minimum wage by nearly 10 percentage points over males (82 percent to 73 percent). This is traceable at least in part to the profile of the minimum wage work force, which has a significant percentage of women. It may also be tied to the fact that women generally approve of social programs in greater numbers than men.[7]

Ethnic and racial divisions stand out clearly. Blacks and Hispanics are much more in favor of a hike than are whites and Asian Americans. The first two groups obviously contain many more people earning the minimum wage or close to it. However, the intense support among African Americans—the highest of any segment of the population—suggests something more than pure self-interested economics may be at work. To many African Americans whose incomes bear no relation to the minimum wage, increasing it may be taken as an important symbolic gesture by the larger society to achieve economic justice. Why otherwise would African American support outstrip Hispanic support? After all, 18 percent of blacks reported in one survey that "someone in their immediate family" earned the minimum wage, while 23 percent of Hispanics said that.[8] Conversely, it is interesting that Asian American support repeatedly falls below that of whites, perhaps because many Asian Americans have a small business orientation or perhaps because they perceive themselves as separate from other minorities.

Socioeconomic variables—education and income—present predictable patterns. Beginning at 82 percent support among those with less than a high school education, backing for minimum wage increases falls steadily to 68 percent among people with postgraduate degrees. Similarly, support reaches 84 percent for those earning under $20,000 but slides to 62 percent at the $75,000 plus level. Interestingly, though, the slope is not as smooth as with the education trend. It drops steadily but slowly from 84 percent to 74 percent through the income levels up to $50,000–74,999 and then falls precipitously among the best-off.

There is only a slight regional variation. In other polls, the East's

Table 4. Group Differences in Support for Raising the Minimum Wage

	"Do you favor or oppose . . . a proposal to raise the minimum wage paid to American workers from $4.25 per hour to $5.15?"		
	Favor an Increase	Oppose an Increase	Not Sure
Gender			
Males	73%	22%	5%
Females	82	15	3
Ethnic/racial category			
Whites	75	21	5
Blacks	95	5	0
Hispanics	89	9	3
Asian Americans	65	21	14
Education level			
Less than high school	82	11	7
High school graduate	80	18	2
Some college	80	16	4
College graduate	70	26	3
Postgraduate degree	68	26	6
Income level			
Less than $20,000	84	13	3
$20,000–34,999	84	13	3
$35,000–49,999	78	18	4
$50,000–74,999	74	25	1
More than $75,000	62	31	7
Regions			
East	79	17	4
Midwest	76	20	4
South	78	17	5
West	77	20	3
Age (years)			
18–29	81	17	2
30–39	80	17	3
40–49	78	20	2
50–64	74	19	7
65 and over	71	20	9
Political party identification			
Democrat	87	10	2
Republican	61	31	9
Independent	81	17	2
Ideological self-identification			
Liberal	88	8	4
Moderate	85	13	2
Conservative	61	33	6

Source: Time/CNN Poll, May 10, 1996.

hairbreadth lead in support opens a bit wider but not by much. Age has a noticeable but fairly modest bearing on how people feel about the issue. The youngest adults—who make up a disproportionate share of the minimum wage earners—are most in favor of the raise. Those in other age brackets are only slightly less supportive, but it does fall to 71 percent among the oldest Americans.

Aside from the gap that separates African Americans and Asian Americans, the greatest disparities are now and always have been in political party identification and self-described ideology. While the magnitudes of the differences across the two categories are roughly the same in this poll, party outweighs ideological identification (but only moderately) in most polls. In this poll, 26 percentage points separate the two major party's foot soldiers, a greater number than in any other category, including income. This is of special moment because it demonstrates that how people orient themselves to the larger political world is sometimes more important in shaping their views than their objective economic circumstances are. Moreover, the political party divide stretches back to the very beginning. In the first poll, asking in 1936 whether people favored a minimum wage constitutional amendment, Democrats' support came in at 84 percent, but Republicans favored it by only 51 percent.

Three generalizations can be drawn from this exercise. First, increasing the minimum wage wins approval from every quarter of the American population. Even the least enthusiastic groups—high-income earners, Republicans, and conservatives—support the increase by a two-to-one margin. Among its weakest backers, a minimum wage increase is still enormously popular.

Second, there are clear signs of self-interest. The inverse relation between both income and educational levels would surprise no one. In the same vein, the pattern depicted by the age brackets shows at least a modicum of self-interest.

Third, notwithstanding the imprint of self-interest, there is a powerful symbolic component to the figures. The inordinately strong support among African Americans is one fact that points to this conclusion. The distinct cleavage between political party and ideological groups, a chasm that supersedes all objective factors, lends further credence to this hypothesis. Support for a minimum wage increase hinges more on political outlook than on class standing or age.

Saliency

Americans display a certain ambivalence about how important the minimum wage is to them. On the one hand, when asked in open-ended questions to identify the most important public problems, the major issues in a campaign, or what they want a president to accomplish, the minimum wage hardly ever breaks the 1 percent threshold. On the other hand, when handed a list of issues or legislative proposals including the minimum wage, people assign it a larger role. Americans also consistently report that a candidate's stand on the minimum wage goes far in determining how they will vote. Yet when called on to specify why they voted for a particular candidate or to elaborate on what the major accomplishments of a presidential administration are, the minimum wage falls to the bottom rungs of the list.

Before each congressional election, the University of Michigan's survey research unit asks the public to name the issues that are important to them in the upcoming election.[9] Invariably, the minimum wage comes in under 1 percent. Also, when the Gallup organization runs its "most important problem" polls, few people mention the minimum wage.[10] Likewise, when President Bush entered office in 1989, the public was asked which problem he should "make an all-out effort to solve first."[11] Raising the minimum wage came in at only 1 percent. Similar results were obtained when people were asked in 1995 what the main "bipartisan agenda" item should be for Congress,[12] or when they were queried about which issues they wanted the candidates to discuss in the 1996 campaign.[13] In each case, all manner of topics took precedence over raising the minimum wage.

When the minimum wage is in the news, however, it moves up the pecking order of issues on the public mind. In August of 1996, as the debate in Congress concluded over an increase in the wage floor, the public was invited to name "the most important thing Bill Clinton has accomplished as president so far."[14] Raising the minimum wage came in third, at 10 percent, behind only welfare reform (15 percent) and improving the economy (12 percent). The next month, a survey plumbed people's feelings about whether the country was headed in the "right" or "wrong" direction and then asked what made the person take that position. Of those who chose the "right direction" option, 10 percent listed the fact that the minimum wage was going up.[15] Falling unemployment took first place with 12 percent, and a host of other issues tied the minimum wage increase at 10 percent (multiple responses were allowed).

When given a list of concerns to choose from, the picture changes decidedly. There are two different types of surveys in which people are asked to select items from a list of issues, and they present different pictures of public sentiment.[16] In one, the person is read a list of issues and asked how important each one is; in the other, people are given a list of issues currently being debated and asked to choose the most or more important issue or sometimes to rank them in some order of importance. The first type of question is designed to tap how important people feel an issue is in isolation from other matters, while the second tries to find out which issues are of greater concern than others. The second exercise is especially enlightening for students of public opinion because it does not allow "cheap" answers. That is, the first type of poll allows the respondent to assign the highest priority to every issue, whereas the second forces a direct choice.

In April of 1996, pollsters read people "a list of national issues Congress is considering" and asked "how important it is to you" that each one be addressed.[17] Respondents were allowed to designate them as "a top priority, a high priority, very important but not a priority, somewhat important, or not important." The results for raising the minimum wage were 18 percent, 18 percent, 27 percent, 22 percent, and 13 percent, respectively. A year before that, Americans were asked whether they would be concerned "a great deal, quite a bit, just some, or not at all," if Congress did not raise the minimum wage.[18] Fully 30 percent said they would be concerned a great deal, another 18 percent said quite a bit, 30 percent indicated moderate concern, and 21 percent were unmoved.

In 1989, a survey provided "a list of actions that could be taken by leaders in business and government" and asked what type of priority—

highest, high, medium, low, or no action at all—should be given to each.[19] Increasing the minimum wage was accorded the highest priority by 21 percent, a high priority by 38 percent, medium priority by 28 percent, and a low priority by only 9 percent, while a mere 5 percent thought no action at all should be taken. Another poll, restricted to those who voted in the 1992 election, used slightly different categories.[20] While reading its list of matters Congress and the president might address, it included a query on whether elevating the minimum wage should be given the single highest priority, made one of the top few, put near the top, assigned a spot in the middle of the list, or relegated to the bottom. The results were 5 percent, 28 percent, 21 percent, 26 percent, and 18 percent, respectively. In every instance, then, when Americans are asked to put a priority on boosting the minimum wage, they say it is highly relevant.

How does increasing the minimum wage stack up against other issues, though? Pollsters periodically compile a list of topics currently before Congress and ask people to identify which "one or two" they feel are the most important. Three of these polls in 1995 included raising the minimum wage, and about one in five people consistently put increasing the minimum wage among their top two priorities (see table 5).

After a president's State of the Union message, a similar poll is often taken, cataloging the issues the president raised in his speech. In

Table 5. Public's Rating of Priorities for Congress

Priorities	January 1995	March 1995	June 1995
Health care reform	29%	40%	45%
Welfare reform	46	41	36
Balance the federal budget	24	30	38
Middle-class tax cut	28	19	17
Crime bill	21	19	17
Increase the minimum wage	18	20	19
Cutting affirmative action	—	7	—
Capital gains tax cut	8	—	—

Sources: NBC News/*Wall Street Journal* Polls, January 17, 1995, March 7, 1995, and June 9, 1995.

Note: Respondents were asked to select "one or two" from a list. The percentages therefore do not equal 100.

1995, Bill Clinton suggested an increase in the minimum wage. In the subsequent poll, people were asked which of his proposals they liked most and if there was another they "liked about as much."[21] Basically, then, they could name two, as in the legislative priorities polls. Again, about one in five listed an increase in the minimum wage in their responses.

Finally, in the poll discussed above about steps business and government leaders might take, the question on priorities was followed by one asking, "Of all the things I just read to you, which is the most important action that could be taken by leaders in business and government?" The minimum wage was second only to cleaning up the environment, although it was far behind that and the choices were severely constrained.[22]

When it comes to voting, the ambivalence continues. Before they cast a vote, people tell pollsters a candidate's position on the minimum wage matters a great deal. In the spring of 1996, for example, prospective voters were asked how important the candidates' stances on various issues were in determining their choice for president.[23] Nineteen percent said the minimum wage was "extremely important," 38 percent indicated "very important," and 29 percent labeled it "somewhat important," while only 14 percent replied that it was not important. Later, during the heat of the campaign, voters were asked how Bob Dole's and Bill Clinton's contrasting positions on the minimum wage might affect their selection.[24] Forty-six percent said they were "much more likely" to support Clinton and 16 percent much more likely to support Dole, while 28 percent considered other issues more important, and 9 percent were not sure.

At the same time, the public was asked, "Suppose your representative in Congress takes a position to favor an increase in the minimum wage. How much would that matter in deciding your vote in the November election?"[25] It mattered a great deal to 23 percent, quite a lot to 15 percent, only some to 36 percent, and not much at all to 26 percent. A converse question, asking how much difference it would make if their member of Congress *opposed* a hike in the minimum wage, provided roughly similar numbers. Of course, these polls did not say *how* it made people vote, for or against, merely that it mattered. Another poll tried to answer that by asking if a candidate for Congress supported raising the minimum wage, would the person be more likely or less likely to cast a vote for the candidate.[26] Twenty-eight percent said they would be much more likely to do so and 39 percent that they would be somewhat more likely, with 7 percent and 9 percent reporting they would be much less and somewhat less likely. Fifteen percent volunteered that it made no difference.

On the surface, then, the minimum wage seemed to be a major factor in both the presidential and congressional elections of 1996. However, when Clinton supporters were asked to name "the main reason" they were voting for Clinton without the prompting of a list, the minimum wage fell to under 1 percent.[27] Even when asked to give the three most important reasons, the minimum wage rose to only 2 percent.[28] In August of 1996, while the minimum wage was being hotly debated in Washington, two different polls asked the public to identify the major accomplishments of the Clinton presidency so far.[29] Increasing the minimum wage gathered 3 percent in one of these and 10 percent in the other, although the second one put it in third place. By January of 1997, however, the president's minimum wage effort had completely faded into the background; only 1 percent listed it as the most important accomplishment of Clinton's first term.[30]

Americans display, in sum, a marked equivocation toward how important the minimum wage is in their political value system and the degree to which it influences their political behavior. They seldom list it on their own as one of the key issues on their political radar screens. Particularly when the question is politically dormant, it recedes to the fringes of public consciousness. However, when expressly placed beside other issues, it rises to what might be characterized as a mid-level item of concern. It does not displace such major topics as the general state of the economy or such broadly popular issues as welfare reform, but it holds its own with such basic matters as crime and tax reform. For a policy that affects such a small number of people, that is not unimportant. As for voting, people claim that a candidate's position on the minimum wage weighs rather heavily on their minds when they enter the polling booth, but there is little direct evidence that it actually does so.

Knowledge and Effects

Over the years, the public has demonstrated a reasonable level of knowledge about the minimum wage program; in fact, it is a striking level, given the minuscule percentage of the population that is directly affected. They seem to believe that the policy has generally beneficial effects, both for the general health of the economy and for various specific groups. Somewhat curiously, a large portion of the public simply does not believe what most economists contend the effects of the minimum wage are.

In the program's early years, several polls asked whether people knew what the term *minimum wage* meant. In the first of these, in 1945, 48 percent gave the correct answer;[31] by 1947, that number had climbed to 68 percent and 77 percent in two different polls.[32] A subsequent poll in the late 1940s provided similar results; the question has not been asked since then.[33]

As for specifying the level of the minimum wage, it depends on whether the person is given a choice. Many people who can identify the correct answer from among several possibilities cannot come up with the figure on their own. A little over 40 percent can usually provide the correct answer unaided, but 86 percent can find it in a multiple choice format.[34]

When asked in 1987 if "an adequate minimum wage is good for the economy," fully 78 percent agreed, 53 percent said "a lot," and 25 percent indicated "a little."[35] Some ten years later, 55 percent were confident that increasing the minimum wage would be an effective way—41 percent very effective and 15 percent fairly effective—to "improve things economically."[36] Furthermore, people believed by a 44 percent to 9 percent margin that raising the minimum wage would make the economy fairer; 42 percent thought it would have no effect, and very few felt the result would be less fair.[37]

The public also seems convinced that raising the minimum wage is a good tool for fighting unemployment. Thirty-seven percent thought in 1994 that increasing the minimum wage would "help a lot" in the "overall job situation," and another 33 percent thought it would "help a little."[38] Conversely, few thought freezing the minimum wage a good idea. Only 4 percent selected that option when given a list of proposals to "reduce unemployment."[39] This compares with 32 percent who chose retraining, the top vote getter.

People see particular groups, beginning with minimum wage workers themselves, as benefiting from a higher minimum wage. Twenty-five percent asserted in 1996 that it was "very likely" that a "meaningful rise in the standard of living of people earning the minimum wage" would result from such an increase, while another 41 percent deemed it "somewhat likely."[40] A proposal to "automatically increase the minimum wage each year to keep pace with inflation" as a way to "help conditions for minorities in urban areas" won the endorsement of 76 percent of the public in 1992.[41] For all that, the public seems somewhat skeptical that increased minimum wage levels will solve the problems of welfare. Although there was broad support (75 percent) for raising the minimum wage "to make work a more attractive alternative to welfare" in 1992,[42] when asked four years later whether "raising the minimum wage would reduce, increase, or not affect" the number of people on welfare, only 26 percent stated that a reduction would result, while 61 percent thought it would have no effect.[43]

One of the more interesting aspects of the public opinion data is that the public seems to be paying little attention to economists. According to a 1978 survey of economists, fully 90 percent believed that higher minimum wages led to unemployment.[44] The question has been put to the public on ten occasions, and in large measure people have voiced serious disagreement with that conclusion.

The general contours of the public's beliefs can be gleaned from a 1996 poll that inquired straightforwardly, "Do you think raising the minimum wage would cost jobs, would create jobs, or would not affect jobs either way?"[45] Nearly half—48 percent—thought it would have no effect, while 33 percent concurred with the economists. Fourteen percent thought, though, that it would actually create jobs. This finding is reinforced by a somewhat different 1993 poll.[46] People were given a chance to rate a variety of government policies on a scale from 0 to 5 for their effect on "the loss of jobs in this country over the past ten years" (0 = no importance; 5 = the greatest importance). One item was whether the minimum wage was too high, which generated the following results: 0 = 30 percent; 1 = 10 percent; 2 = 19 percent; 3 = 15 percent; 4 = 7 percent; 5 = 10 percent; don't know = 1 percent.

Neither is the public convinced that higher minimum wages necessarily hurt various groups of people working at the minimum wage. The three polls dealing with "unskilled" and "low wage" workers present a somewhat mixed picture. The seemingly contradictory results, however, may relate to how the questions were worded. In a 1996 poll, people were asked whether they agreed or disagreed "that raising the minimum wage would make it harder for low-wage workers to find jobs, because employers would hire fewer people."[47] Only 31 percent agreed, and 69 percent disagreed. But when the idea was put a different way in another 1996 poll—"Would fewer jobs for unskilled workers be very likely, somewhat likely, or not very likely to result from a higher minimum wage?"—the outcome was rather different.[48] Thirty-eight percent thought it not very likely, the largest single response category, but 34 percent felt it somewhat likely and 25 percent very likely. A poll conducted in 1981 found results lying between these two.[49] After informing the respondent that the minimum wage had just gone up, the interviewer continued, "Some people say that each time the minimum wage is raised, many low wage earners lose jobs because some employers cannot afford to pay the higher minimum wage. Do you generally agree or generally disagree with this statement?" Forty-nine percent disagreed, and 44 percent agreed. Although each of these polls presents a different picture of the public's views on how jobs for low-wage workers are affected by the minimum wage, they all show a view sharply at variance with that of professional economists. At the very least, nearly 40 percent of Americans think higher minimum wages have no adverse effect on the job prospects of those with few skills.

There is a more clear-cut consensus on the employment effects for young people and minorities. In 1979 and 1981, the public was asked an identical question: "Some people say when the minimum wage goes up it means fewer jobs for young people. Others say this isn't true, that it just means young people get paid better for what they do. What do you think happens when the minimum wage goes up—that there are fewer jobs for young people or that it just means better pay for them?"[50] The results were quite similar; 71 percent in 1979 and 65 percent in

1981 believed it just meant fatter paychecks for young workers. A poll from 1980 sheds further light on this issue.[51] People were handed a list of nine possible causes of "the high unemployment rate among young people" and "among young Blacks." Not being "good enough to be worth the new minimum wage" came in eighth place for both groups, at 15 percent for the former and 12 percent for the latter.

There is one poll that ran decidedly the other way, however, on the general issue of employment.[52] The question (asked in 1987) elicited an "agree a lot" to "disagree a lot" choice to the statement "Raising the minimum wage might result in some job loss." Fifty-four percent registered agreement with the statement, 24 percent a lot and 30 percent a little; 41 percent disagreed, 19 percent a little and 22 percent a lot. Although a majority agreed that job loss might occur, it is worth noting that four in ten people still dissented from economic orthodoxy.

Self-Interest versus a Sense of Community

The individualist view of politics has it that people are guided largely if not entirely by self-interest in their political attitudes and behavior. Civic republicanism, in contrast, contends that Americans have a sense of concern, varying from weak to strong depending on the writer, for their fellow citizens and that they feel a bond with the larger community. Is there a discernible tilt toward one of these poles running through public attitudes when it comes to the minimum wage?

It is quite clear that there is a shadow of self-interest in the structure of public opinion regarding the minimum wage. Backing for a higher minimum wage was found to be more pronounced among women, lower-income earners, the less educated, the young, and minorities— all groups that, as the following chapter makes abundantly clear, contribute more than their share of people to the minimum wage work force. Nevertheless, there is also compelling evidence that the public's views on the minimum wage contain a strong strain of communitarian values. Five features of public opinion support this conclusion.

First, there is the general backing for minimum wage increases. While such advocacy is certainly greater among those most affected, the data can be read a different way. The sheer magnitude of the favorable response to hiking the minimum wage is one bit of evidence that the public is not locked into self-interest alone. Between 8 and 20 percent of people report a minimum wage worker in their family.[53] At the very least, then, 80 percent of the public has no direct monetary stake in a minimum wage increase. Even if everyone who is supposedly remotely touched by the minimum wage were in favor of seeing it raised, a substantial majority of the rest of the population would also have to view an increase favorably to produce the poll numbers. Simply put, if 80 percent are unaffected, then 75 percent of them would have to be in favor for the 80 percent overall figure to be reached. A second piece of evidence is that even among the groups most directly affected, nothing near a majority of the people composing those categories toil at the minimum wage. Many women and minorities, for example, are clearly showing concern for people other than themselves. Finally, it cannot be stressed too often that a *majority* of every group favors a higher minimum wage. Even among those with absolutely nothing to gain (people whose income exceeds $75,000) and those ideologically committed to pro-business and pro-market positions, support for a minimum wage increase routinely runs over 60 percent.

Second, Americans often accord as high a priority to minimum wage increases as they do to policies that would help them. Consider, for example, the three legislative priorities polls summarized in table 5. In the March and June surveys, increasing the minimum wage held its own or even slightly topped any clamor for a middle-class tax cut. In the January poll, it fell somewhat behind middle-class tax relief but still outpaced a capital gains tax cut by a wide margin. Going back to late 1960, the public was given a list of twenty items and asked to indicate its preferred priorities for the incoming president and Congress (multiple responses were allowed).[54] "Raising the minimum wage to $1.25" came in third place, 6 percentage points ahead of "reducing taxes for people like myself."

Third, every time people are asked, they voice a desire that the minimum wage be higher than Congress cares to set it. During the 1989 debate, three polls probed whether the raise should be to $4.25 or to $4.55 (from $3.35).[55] In each, about two-thirds of those favoring an increase opted for the higher figure. In 1994, when the law provided for $4.25, the public was asked what the minimum wage should be.[56] The mean of all responses was $5.80. In 1996, as Congress completed action raising the minimum wage to $5.15 in two steps, the public spoke its mind through a poll that offered several brackets ranging from $3.20–4.00 to over $6.25.[57] While 25 percent selected $4.76–5.00, in line with the first of the soon-to-be-enacted slated increases, 38 percent would have preferred amounts over $5.26, with 15 percent going for a minimum wage of over $6.25. This was the second largest cohort, as shown in table 6. This pattern stretches back to the 1940s.[58]

The public clearly knows that one cannot support oneself, much less a family, on the minimum wage.[59] Apparently, though, people think one should be able to do so. When asked in 1987 whether "employers should pay a full time worker enough for the worker and his or her family to survive without public assistance," 62 percent "agreed a lot," and 19 percent seconded that by agreeing "a little."[60] When quizzed in 1989 whether they favored or opposed "a minimum wage high enough so that a family of four could live above the poverty line if the father worked and the mother stayed home," 75 percent said they favored this, while only a paltry 17 percent opposed it.[61] Conceptually, then, Americans seem to want the minimum wage to approach a living wage.

It should be noted that these beliefs come into conflict with the ideology of the market. A 1987 poll wanted to know whether people

Table 6. What the Minimum Wage Should Be (1996)

"As you know the federal government establishes a minimum wage in this country, which requires employers to pay at least a certain amount per hour to their workers. What do you think the minimum wage per hour should be?"

None	2%	$5.26–5.50	9%
$3.20–4.00	1	$5.51–5.75	3
$4.01–4.25	6	$5.76–6.00	10
$4.26–4.50	3	$6.01–6.25	1
$4.51–4.75	2	More than $6.25	15
$4.76–5.00	25	Don't know	6
$5.01–5.25	10		

Source: CNN/*USA Today* Poll, May 12, 1996.
Note: The minimum wage at the time was $4.25.

agreed that "wage levels should be set by the market and not by the government."[62] Forty-nine percent agreed "a lot," and 20 percent agreed "a little." There is a degree of double-mindedness here also. Many people, however, may have been answering in general, since the question did not refer specifically to those in low-wage occupations, which means the results were not necessarily in conflict with support for a relatively high minimum wage.

A fourth bit of evidence for the community-interest position can be found when the minimum wage crops up in polls about general values. In 1996, the University of Virginia conducted an intensive study of American public values, called the Post-Modernity Project.[63] Among the questions was the following: "We can also look at specific situations where the expression of personal freedom might harm the larger community. For each of the following situations, please state the number that best reflects which you think should take priority—individual freedom or the public good. (1)Individual freedom has much greater priority; (2) Individual freedom has greater priority; (3) Both have equal priority; (4) The public good has greater priority; (5) The public good has much greater priority. Which takes priority when the owner of a small business ignores the minimum wage, arguing that he should be free to pay employees whatever he can afford?" The result of this inquiry was 7 percent for choice number 1, 10 percent for number 2, 16 percent for number 3, 31 percent for number 4, and 36 percent for number 5. In short, 67 percent settled on the public good, and of those, a majority said the interests of the public were much greater than the need for individual freedom. Of course, this answer profile may reflect attitudes about illegal behavior as much as support for the minimum wage itself. Another survey in 1995, however, pointed to a high level of civic consciousness regarding the minimum wage.[64] When given a stark rendition of the minimum wage's possible effects, nearly two-thirds still embraced raising it. The exact wording of the question was "Some people have suggested that the minimum wage be increased to help people in low-paying jobs keep up with the cost of living. Other people feel that an increase in the minimum wage would increase costs to businesses and weaken the economy. Do you favor or oppose increasing the minimum wage?" The responses were 64 percent in favor, 31 percent opposed, and 5 percent not sure.

A fifth and final pillar for supposing that a communitarian ethos survives can be found when attitudes about the minimum wage's direct costs are solicited. Some critics of minimum wage opinion polls, particularly the type discussed in the first section of this chapter, which ask only for a favor/oppose opinion, argue that they are misleading because they present no costs. That is, people can say they favor a minimum wage hike without having to assess any tradeoffs. This is an empty criticism.

First, the public is well aware that minimum wage increases carry costs. People were asked in 1996 if they thought "raising the minimum wage would increase prices for consumers, would lower prices, or would not affect prices either way."[65] Fully 62 percent said they thought it would increase prices. Moreover, the public is willing to grant that small businesses might suffer. Twenty-five percent, for example, said it was very likely and 43 percent somewhat likely that financial problems for small businesses would flow from a minimum wage increase.[66] When 75–80 percent declare they wish to see a minimum wage hike, they are not unaware of its potential costs.

But what if they were presented with the costs in the same question? Conceivably, if people are asked about the desirability of a policy at one point and about its costs at another, they may not connect the two in their minds. When the two are combined, however, one cannot forget or ignore. Fortunately, several polls do just that, the results of which clinch the case.

The most graphic evidence may be from a 1989 poll that asked those who favored a minimum wage hike if they would "still favor raising the minimum wage even if businesses passed the increased salary costs along to the American consumer in the form of higher prices on some goods and services."[67] A resounding 82 percent said yes, indicating that they were willing to pay these costs so that minimum wage workers could have a wage increase. Another poll put the price increase issue equally directly:[68] "Keeping in mind that any increase would likely result in a slight increase in the costs of goods and services, what do you think the hourly minimum wage should be?" The mean response was 36 percent above the then current minimum wage.

Buttressing this finding is a poll that asked about a person's priorities "even if it means increased taxes."[69] Increasing the minimum wage remained a top priority for 26 percent and a very important priority for an additional 41 percent of the respondents. The sample for this poll was adult women, but even if men's numbers caused these figures to slip somewhat, the public seems ready to pay higher taxes so that minimum wage workers can benefit.

That the public is concerned about the fate of minimum wage workers can be seen from a companion question to the 1989 query on price increases. It asked, "Would you still favor raising the minimum wage even if it causes some businesses to fire workers or stop hiring workers rather than pay the increased salary?" Support fell to 52 percent still in favor (although 3 percent volunteered that they did not think that would happen), compared with the 82 percent prepared to pay higher consumer prices. Unquestionably, people care more for the interests of minimum wage workers than they care about a small raid on their own pocketbooks.

In other polls, concern about the employment outlook for those working at the minimum wage is also evident. Depending on how strongly the question is worded, the results fluctuate. This is probably tied to how probable the public thinks job loss will be. When the wording is somewhat soft, support for minimum wage increases remains over 50 percent. For example, a 1996 poll asked, "Would you still favor an increase in the minimum wage if it *might* reduce the number of jobs available for workers with limited skills?"[70] Of those with an opinion, 55 percent were still in favor. If the proposition is stated as a certainty, though, people have second thoughts. Another 1996 poll asked, "Now thinking about the current debate on the minimum wage. Would you favor or oppose raising the minimum wage if it *resulted* in fewer jobs available to low paid workers in this country?"[71] Given this thrust, 41 percent of those with an opinion still favored the increase.

In short, people seem willing to shift the burden of a minimum wage increase to themselves in the form of either higher prices or increased taxes, but they are hesitant to hurt low-wage workers. That can only be testimony to an enduring and admirable humanitarianism and civic consciousness, two central values of civic republicanism, running through the public psyche. The groundwork is there for approaching the minimum wage from the perspective of the political economy of citizenship.

4

The Sociology of the Minimum Wage

It is always important to remember that regulatory policies, even ones whose politics are symbolic, when implemented affect real people. Government reports or graphs reflecting economic theory can easily mask the human side of the story. Academics and policy analysts are particularly prone to pore over surveys and data compilations, seeing in them alone the results of public policies. Most of what follows in this chapter comes from these usual sources, but I tried to balance that by supplementing the data with conversations with people with faces, names, and histories.

The best statistical source of data on minimum wage workers is the Current Population Survey, conducted by the Bureau of Labor Statistics.[1] There are some technical conceptual problems with using these data to generalize about the minimum wage work force, but they are relatively minor.[2] When these data are compared with more qualitative studies, the outlines tend to hold up well.

An Overview

In the second quarter of 1997, before the minimum wage rose from $4.75 to $5.15 per hour (on September 1, 1997), nearly 1.5 million people earned exactly the minimum wage, and another 4.9 million earned between $4.76 and $5.14 an hour. Together, this group made up 5 percent of the total civilian work force and 9 percent of workers paid by the hour.[3] It is also approximately 25 out of every 1,000 Americans. Since the demographic profile of both minimum wage workers and those near the minimum wage is about the same, the data on the minimum wage workers are used to fashion a collective portrait of these people.

The popular image of minimum wage workers is high school and college students flipping and serving burgers, and the statistics bear that out to some degree. Thirty-four percent of these 1.5 million people are between the ages of 16 and 19, and another 21 percent are between 20 and 24 years old. Conversely, though, that means that 45 percent are over 24. It is equally revealing that while 59 percent work part-time, 41 percent are employed full-time (see table 7).[4]

The racial and ethnic composition of the minimum wage work force is rather difficult to ascertain since people give multiple answers to such questions. This is particularly true for Hispanics, who often classify themselves as "white" or give a subgroup label, such as "Mexican" or "Puerto Rican." For all minimum wage workers, 87 percent claimed to be white, 10 percent black, and 3 percent other. Hispanics, who were distributed over all three of these groups, made up 22 percent. In the analyses presented below, I confine myself to contrasting whites and blacks and then provide a note on Hispanics at the end.

Table 7. The Minimum Wage Work Force

	Percentage
Age (years)	
16–19	34
20–24	21
25 and over	45
Employment status	
Part-time	59
Full-time	41
Ethnic/racial category	
White	87
Black	10
Other	3
Gender	
Male	42
Female	58
Marital status	
Never married	60
Married, living with spouse	26
Separated/divorced/widowed	14

Source: Current Population Survey, Second Quarter 1997.

Women are disproportionately represented, contributing 58 percent of the minimum wage worker pool. Sixty percent of both sexes have never been married, while 26 percent are currently married and living with their spouses. A vast majority, 79 percent, work in "service-producing" industries, with a concentration in the retail trade area. Further, there are pronounced regional patterns. Minimum wage workers constitute nearly 6 percent of the hourly paid work force in Louisiana, for example, but only one-third of 1 percent in New Hampshire and Oregon.[5] With this general picture in mind, we can now take a closer look at these people.

Age

Minimum wage workers are relatively young: 55 percent are under 25, and over a third of the total are between 16 and 19. Women minimum wage workers tend to be older, however. Fifty-two percent of the 16–19 age group are men, but only 32 percent of the over 24 segment are. It is unclear whether women are staying in minimum wage jobs longer, whether the types of jobs women hold are more likely to be lower paid, or whether they are entering the work force later.[6] The racial breakdown remains constant throughout the age brackets, about 93–95 percent white and 5–7 percent African American.

Of the 16–19 cohort, 49 percent are white males and 43 percent white females. Black males constitute only 3 percent of this group and black females 4 percent. Among white teenagers, males outnumber females 53 percent to 47 percent in the minimum wage job market, while for African Americans, females are dominant over males, 57 percent females and 43 percent males.

When people move to the next age level, the overall division between males and females evens out, but the racial disparity becomes even greater. Of all minimum wage workers who are between 20 and 24, white men make up 48 percent and white women 44 percent (see table 8). Black males are only 1 percent of this group, but black women are 5 percent. Among whites in this age group, 52 percent are men and 48 percent women, while among blacks, 83 percent are women and

Table 8. Minimum Wage Workers by Age, Race, and Gender

	Age (Years)		
	16–19	20–24	Over 25
White males	49%	48%	23%
White females	43	44	56
Black males	3	1	7
Black females	4	5	9

Source: Current Population Survey, Second Quarter 1997.

only 17 percent are men. The low percentage of black males in this group is one of the most puzzling aspects of the demographics of the minimum wage work force.

In the 25 and over group—which, remember, makes up 45 percent of the minimum wage pool—the proportion of white males drops dramatically, to only 23 percent. White females contribute 56 percent, black males 7 percent, and black females 9 percent. For whites, then, the proportion shifts in favor of females, 71 percent females and 29 percent males; blacks return to roughly the percentages found while they were teenagers, 57 percent female and 43 percent male.

There are equally interesting patterns among middle-age people, those 35–44 and 45–54. First, the number of people working at the minimum wage drops quickly over age 25.[7] Where 312,000 minimum wage workers are found in the 20–24 bracket, only 128,000 are between 25 and 29, a drop of more than 50 percent. For the ten-year age bracket of 35–44, there are 198,000, a total that falls by over 50 percent, to 98,000, by the time people reach 45–54.

As for the gender and racial composition of the 35–44 segment, it betrays an unmistakable black male and white female cast. White males constitute 14 percent of this group, white females 68 percent, black males 11 percent, and black females 8 percent. This means that 83 percent of the white workers in this age group are female and that 58 percent of the blacks are male. Moreover, since black males make up about 7 percent of the total population and white females about 44 percent, the 11 percent and 68 percent figures mean these two groups are vastly overrepresented among minimum wage workers between 35 and 44.

While the inordinately large number of white females can probably be explained by women entering the job market after their children reach school age, the reason for the high black male corps is not at all clear. Perhaps, given the low number found in the early years, many are entering the job market late. It is well to remember, though, that even among men, white men still contribute larger absolute numbers than do black men: 54 percent of the men in this age group are white.

The configuration shifts again when late middle age approaches. The number of white men stays about the same; white women and black men exit the group; and black women enter in droves. All this alters the percentages each category contributes to this cohort, even though the overall sex breakdown remains largely undisturbed at 28 percent male. White males now contribute 24 percent overall, which is 34 percent of the whites and 85 percent of the males. White females make up 46 percent of the total, which is 66 percent of the whites and 64 percent of the females. Black men make up only 4 percent overall and only 14 percent of the blacks. Black females are the only group to grow in absolute numbers—at a steep 71 percent rate. This gives them a 26 percent presence in this age group. The reasons behind this flood of African American women in the minimum wage job market are hazy.

Race

Significant racial differences can be gleaned from the data presented above. However, we can also view race from a different angle, breaking down various categories of people by race. If we do so, we find that on the whole, black minimum wage workers tend to be older than whites, that a greater percentage of them work full-time, and that the black work force is more female dominated than the white work force is (see table 9).

Among white minimum wage workers, 37 percent are 16–19, 22 percent are 20–24, and 41 percent are over 24. These figures stand in sharp contrast to the 22 percent of black minimum wage workers who are 16–19, the 10 percent who are 20–24, and the 68 percent who are 25 or over. Whites seem to go to work much earlier, particularly in

Table 9. Minimum Wage Workers by Race

	White	Black
Age (years)		
16–19	37%	22%
20–24	22	10
25 and over	41	68
Employment status		
Part-time	62	45
Full-time	38	55
Gender		
Male	43	39
Female	57	61

Source: Current Population Survey, Second Quarter 1997.

the 20–24 bracket, but blacks seem to be locked in the minimum wage treadmill much longer. Fully two-thirds of blacks who hold a minimum wage job are 25 or over.

Blacks are also much more likely to work full-time, which is no doubt tied to these age patterns. Fifty-five percent of black minimum wage workers toil full-time, but only 38 percent of whites do. Apparently, large numbers of white youths are taking part-time jobs in high school and college and leaving them as they mature. Many more blacks are mired in minimum wage jobs as a permanent part of their work lives.

The gender divisions are also skewed by race. Overall, 57 percent of white minimum wage workers are females, but 61 percent of blacks are. From these figures, middle-aged black women working at the minimum wage are clearly a critical element of the minimum wage work force.

Gender

Partitioning the minimum wage work force by gender reveals that over-all its female portion is generally older and has a greater tendency to work part-time. For men, 42 percent can be found in the 16–19 age group, 24 percent are between 20 and 24, and 33 percent are over 24. For women, the comparable percentages are 29 percent, 18 percent, and 53 percent. Over half the women are 25 and over, and 37 percent are 35 and over. At least for women, the image of teenage cashiers working at retail stores and fast-food restaurants is simply off the mark.

A little over half of the men in the minimum wage work force, 53 percent, work part-time, whereas 64 percent of the women do. This is interesting, for one thing, because it is usually teenagers who leap to mind when part-time minimum wage workers are mentioned. Yet the age skew for women means that substantial numbers of adult women are working part-time. It also means that nearly half the men are working full-time. If many of the younger group of males are employed part-time, surely a reasonable assumption, then many of the adult men must be contributing a large portion of a family's income through full-time minimum wage jobs.

The overall racial divisions are very similar for men and women, about 90 percent white in both cases. However, this composite figure masks important differences among the various age groups, as discussed above.

Part-Time and Full-Time Work

When it comes to sorting out the full-time and part-time components of the minimum wage work force, what is hinted at above becomes evident.[8] Of all the full-time minimum wage workers, 81 percent are white, and 51 percent are female. For part-timers, 92 percent are white, and 62 percent are women.

Contrary to most people's images, white men make up 41 percent of the full-time minimum wage work force. White women contribute 40 percent. Black men are 6 percent of the full-timers and black women 8 percent. The part-time minimum wage work force is heavily dominated by white females. Fully 56 percent of part-timers are white women, while 35 percent are white men. Black men are 3 percent and black women 5 percent. These numbers are closely tied to the age breakdown, which indicated few young black males in the minimum wage work force. If males take more part-time jobs between their sixteenth and nineteenth birthdays than they do full-time ones, then black males will make up less of the part-time minimum wage work force than they otherwise would, given their relative absence from the 16–

19 and 20–24 age groups. Since white men are 41 percent of the total minimum wage work force and 45 percent of them work full-time, these full-time white male workers are 17 percent—nearly one in five—of the entire population of minimum wage workers. Again, this is not the picture most people carry around in their heads.

Marital Status

Minimum wage workers tend to be single, which is again undoubtedly tied to age. Sixty percent have never been married, a figure that rises to 94 percent among those 16–24. A little over a quarter, 26 percent, are living with their spouses. Fifty-one percent of those 25 and over live with a spouse. Only 8 percent of minimum wage workers are separated or divorced, but 17 percent of those over 24 are.

There are conspicuous differences between men and women in this regard. Taking all males together, 74 percent have never been married, showing the statistical effects of the large number of males 16–19 years old. Of men in the youngest age cluster, 97 percent have never been married. For men who have been married, though, it is very likely that a spouse is present. Of those married at least once, 77 percent are currently living with their spouses. A bare 4 percent of the men overall and 15 percent of those married at least once are divorced or separated.

In contrast, only 50 percent of the women have never been married, which undoubtedly reflects the age differences uncovered above concerning when women enter the minimum wage work force. Ninety-one percent of the women between 16 and 24, not far from the male figure, have never been married, but only 14 percent of those over 24 have not. Women have a lower rate of intact marriages, however. For those who have been married, 61 percent are living with a spouse. While 12 percent of the remainder are widowed (whereas virtually no males are), the rest are separated or divorced. The smaller number of women who are currently married may contain a clue as to why we saw a bulge in women 35–44 working at the minimum wage; many may be going to work or taking a second job after a divorce or a spouse's death.

An Occupational Profile

The occupational structure of the minimum wage work force is largely what anyone would expect, although there are some interesting aspects to note.

First, 93 percent of all minimum wage workers are in the private sector. Among the handful who work in the public sector, 50 percent work for local governments, 38 percent for states, and only 12 percent for the federal government. More women than men work for governments; 8 percent of the women but only 5 percent of the men are employed in public service. Since local governments are the main employers of minimum wage workers in the public sector, school cafeteria and other service workers probably make up a significant number of these people.

In the private sector, what the government labels "service-producing" industries absorb the vast bulk of minimum wage workers. Manufacturing, the original target of the Fair Labor Standards Act, employs 15 percent of the men and 8 percent of the women, for a total of 11 percent. Agriculture embraces 5 percent of the men and a bare 1 percent of the women, for an overall total of 3 percent. Service-producing businesses, by contrast, provide employment for 79 percent of all minimum wage workers and 85 percent of those located in the private sector.

"Service producing" is a diverse category, however, encompassing everything from shoe repair shops, grocery stores, wholesale office supply dealers, and janitorial services firms to real estate agencies, lawyers, and computer consultants. Retail trade, a subcategory of service producing, is home to 50 percent of all minimum wage workers, and half of those, 24 percent overall, work in eating and drinking establishments. While your fast-food order-taker, preparer, and cashier are part of the largest single component of the minimum wage work force, they are far from a majority.

Women outnumber men in the wholesale and retail trade sector but only slightly.[9] Approximately 57 percent of the people working here are women. But, since there are more women than men in the total minimum wage work force, these workers form identical percentages of the men and women minimum wage workers. Men who work in wholesale and retail trade are 52 percent of all male minimum wage workers, as are their female coworkers.

The only other place where significant gender differences appear is in professional services. Women outnumber men four to one in this sector, probably because many women work in entry-level clerical occupations. Since the total for professional services is less than 8 percent of the overall minimum wage work force, though, the number of people involved is quite small.

The occupational categories used by the Department of Labor, as opposed to the industrial sectors, provide additional useful information. Sixty-one percent of all minimum wage workers are in "services, except household and protective" and "sales occupations." If we add three other job titles, we can account for 88 percent of the minimum wage work force (see table 10).

The gender division is predictable. A higher percentage of women than men occupy jobs in the service, sales, and clerical fields. One noteworthy item is that 30 percent of the men hold jobs as either "machine operators, assemblers, and inspectors" or "handlers, equipment cleaners, helpers, and laborers." These are positions largely hidden from public view, unlike restaurant workers. Perhaps many of the older men who are working full-time are in this set.

Table 10. Occupations of Minimum Wage Workers

	Percentage of		
Occupation	All Workers	Men	Women
Service, except household and			
protective	38	35	39
Sales occupations	23	13	31
Machine operators, assemblers,			
and inspectors	10	14	7
Administrative support, including			
clerical	9	3	14
Handlers, equipment cleaners, helpers,			
and laborers	8	16	2

Source: Current Population Survey, Second Quarter 1997.

The Regional Factor

A fourth of the country's minimum wage workers are in two states, Texas and California. Approximately another third live in eight other states. Of course, most of these states have fairly large populations, but they are not in rank order of population by any means, as shown in table 11. Louisiana and Washington are particularly out of place.

Tables 12 and 13 show the ten states with the highest number of minimum wage workers as a percentage of the hourly paid work force and per 10,000 residents, respectively. Only Arizona and Kentucky do not appear on both lists. Except for Montana's move from eighth to fourth, though, the ranks pretty much hold. Arizona was nowhere near making the first list, although Kentucky was close to being included on the second. Arizona's unusual position is explained by two facts, the first of which is the high percentage of hourly paid workers in its economy. In Arizona, 32 percent of the population are hourly paid workers, whereas nationally 27 percent are. A smaller percentage of the hourly work force could therefore be a larger than normal percentage of the population as a whole. The second is that in Arizona, more hourly workers than normal earn premium wages. In the second quar-

Table 11. Top Ten States for Number of Minimum Wage Workers

State	Number (Thousands)	Percentage of National Minimum Wage Work Force	Population Rank
Texas	221	14.7	2
California	143	9.5	1
New York	109	7.3	3
Ohio	92	6.1	7
Pennsylvania	77	5.1	5
Florida	76	5.1	4
Louisiana	60	4.0	21
Illinois	52	3.5	6
Michigan	44	2.9	8
Washington	39	2.6	15
Totals	913	60.9	

Source: Current Population Survey, Second Quarter 1997.

Table 12. Ten States with the Highest Percentage of
Hourly Paid Workers Earning the Minimum Wage

State	Percentage
Wyoming	11.5
Louisiana	5.9
West Virginia	4.7
Arkansas	4.7
North Dakota	4.6
Mississippi	4.4
Texas	4.4
Montana	4.4
New Mexico	3.7
Kentucky	3.7

Source: Current Population Survey, Second Quarter 1997.

Table 13. Ten States with the Highest Number of
Minimum Wage Workers per 10,000 Residents

State	Number
Wyoming	31.5
Louisiana	13.8
West Virginia	13.1
Montana	12.6
North Dakota	12.5
Arkansas	12.1
Texas	11.8
Mississippi	11.5
New Mexico	9.5
Arizona	8.5

Source: Current Population Survey, Second Quarter 1997.

ter of 1997, 88.3 percent of its hourly workers made $5.15 and above, while the national average stood at 87.6 percent. This would drive down the percentage of the hourly paid work force making the minimum wage.

If we search for common characteristics among these eleven states, two things seem to stand out: poverty and tourists' destinations. Louisiana, West Virginia, Arkansas, Kentucky, North Dakota, and Mississippi are all relatively poor, and Arkansas and Kentucky, at least, can also boast a dollop of tourist trade. Wyoming, Montana, and Arizona have substantial tourism sectors in their economies. New Mexico and large patches of Texas fall into both categories. In most cases, these are nonurban states, and all except West Virginia and North Dakota are in the South or the West.

The fit is not perfect, however. Some traditionally poor states—such as Alabama and South Carolina—are not on the list. Plus, some popular tourist destinations, even outside the East, such as Colorado and Utah, do not land in the group. Many rural states are not on the list either.

In sum, if we want to find the greatest number of minimum wage workers, we should head to Texas and California. If we want to find them more frequently, we can go to Wyoming, Louisiana, and West Virginia.

A Note on Hispanics

Twenty-two percent of all minimum wage workers designate themselves as Hispanics or one of the subcategories that make up this segment of the American population.[10] The profile of these people is manifestly different from that of both black and white Americans who work for minimum wages.

First, the gender split is even, exactly 50 percent for each (see table 14). Second, these workers are older. Sixty percent of them are 25 and over,

Table 14. Hispanic Minimum Wage Workers

	Percentage
Gender	
Men	50
Women	50
Age (years)	
16–19	12
20–24	28
25 and over	60
Employment status	
Full-time	65
Part-time	35

Source: Current Population Survey, Second Quarter 1997.

with only 12 percent between 16 and 19, and 28 percent falling into the 20–24 band. Moreover, there are emphatic age differences between Hispanic men and women. Only 6 percent of the men are 16–19 years old, with 40 percent 20–24, and 54 percent 25 and over. For women, 19 percent are 16–19, 16 percent 20–24, and 66 percent over 24.

The most startling difference, however, is in the hours worked. Sixty-five percent of Hispanic minimum wage workers are full-time employees. Slicing further, only half the women work full-time, but 80 percent of the men do. A detailed breakdown by age, gender, and full-time/part-time status is not available from the Bureau of Labor Statistics' figures, but if 54 percent of the men are over 24 and 80 percent of all men are working full-time, there are obviously many Hispanic men toiling full-time for very low wages. It also seems reasonable to infer that a substantial number of that 17 percent of "white males" we discovered working full-time might be these Hispanics. Recall, too, the large percentages of minimum wage workers in Texas and California, states with sizable Hispanic populations. Perhaps these full-time Hispanic men are also many of the "machine operators, assemblers, and inspectors" and "handlers, equipment cleaners, helpers, and laborers" that compose nearly one-third of the male minimum wage work force. If so, is this a group of our fellow citizens who are almost invisible when debates are held on the minimum wage?

The Families of Minimum Wage Workers

As part of its 1996 survey of adults 18 and over regarding the minimum wage, the Associated Press asked, "Does someone in your immediate family earn just the minimum wage?"[11] With a question like this, of course, it could be anyone from a teenager working a few hours a week to a major breadwinner. It gives us a starting point different from the Current Population Survey, which deals with individuals. Seventeen percent answered the query in the affirmative. Even though under 1 percent of the population labors at the minimum wage, it touches nearly one in every five American families, assuming the answers were accurate.

It is extraordinary that 11 percent of the males but 22 percent of the females replied yes to the question (see table 15). This is intriguing because even though more women than men work at the minimum wage, it would not seem to affect families this disproportionately. Is this a reflection of the large number of female-headed households? Or are many women who live alone working at the minimum wage? A racial distribution discloses that 15 percent of whites, 18 percent of blacks, but 23 percent of Hispanics have a minimum wage worker in the family. Although black families will be affected more than white families by a change in minimum wage policy, the Hispanic community is the one most affected. Nearly one in four Hispanic families in this country contains a minimum wage worker; and recall that, according to the Current Population Survey, four out of five male Hispanic minimum wage workers, half of all the Hispanics, work full-time.

It is often alleged that many minimum wage earners are middle-class teenagers just earning a little spending money—the lawyer's son who wants a better CD player for his car. But that is not the picture that emerges here. Well-educated, prosperous people seldom send their teens off to bag groceries or cook pizzas. Only 7 percent of adults with a postgraduate degree and 9 percent who are college graduates have a minimum wage worker in the family. In contrast, 23 percent of adults who are not high school graduates, 17 percent who went no further than high school, and 20 percent of those with some college live in a family where someone earns just the minimum wage. The income skew is just as sobering. Thirteen percent of families enjoying an income over $50,000 contain a minimum wage worker, but 32 percent of those in the under $15,000 bracket and 20 percent of those in the $15,000–19,999 segment do. The teenager working at the fast-food restaurant is therefore probably the son or daughter of a working-class family, more likely earning money for school clothes than for a new CD player.

As for age, it is young and middle-age adults who have minimum wage workers in their families. Twenty-three percent of those 18–29 years old do, and 20 percent of the 40–49 bracket do. Many of the first group must be referring to themselves, while many of the second are surely parents of minimum wage workers. The lowest groups are

Table 15. Americans with a Minimum Wage
Worker in Their Immediate Families

	Percentage
Gender	
Males	11
Females	22
Ethnic/racial category	
White	16
Black	18
Hispanic	23
Education level	
Less than high school	23
High school graduate	17
Some college	20
College graduate	9
Postgraduate degree	7
Income level	
Less than $15,000	32
$15,000–19,999	20
$20,000–29,999	17
$30,000–49,999	12
More than $50,000	13
Age (years)	
18–29	23
30–39	11
40–49	20
50–59	17
60–69	16
70 and over	10
Region	
East	19
Midwest	13
South	18
West	17
Political party identification	
Republican	15
Democrat	16
Independent	20

Source: Associated Press Poll, May 1996.
Note: Two percent answered they did not know.

30–3 8 (1 1 percent) and 70 and over (1 0 percent). The first group has likely largely moved out of the minimum wage work force and is too young to have teenage children; the second probably has few young people in immediate families. Still, one in ten older Americans is closely related to a minimum wage worker.

The regional pattern is rather surprising considering the state figures provided earlier. The largest number of affected families is found in the East, not the South or the West, although the spread is so small it could result from the margin of error. Assuming these three regions are roughly on par, it is still most puzzling. Could the small percentages of the work force we saw in the East generally come from quite large families? Do the seemingly high-income economies of the East Coast mask a segment of people still mired in low-wage jobs? How else can we square the fact that nearly one in five people in the East reports a minimum wage worker in the family?

One final item of interest from the survey is the political party figures. They are nearly identical. Fifteen percent of Republicans and 1 6 percent of Democrats see a minimum wage worker when they sit at the family dinner table. The differences in their feelings about the minimum wage reported in the previous chapter therefore do not come from a lack of personal contact with people holding minimum wage jobs.

A Day at the Employment Office

To get perspective on the contemporary minimum wage, I spent a day at the local employment office, officially the Mississippi Employment Security Commission (MESC). I interviewed the office manager, the placement supervisor, and two interviewers. I sat in, with the permission of the applicants, on a number of interviews. They were informed I was working on a research project on the minimum wage and asked if they minded if I attended the interview. Only one said he preferred not. Although I did not question them or initiate any conversation, several of the applicants chatted with me voluntarily, especially during the frequent telephone interruptions. I sat for a while in the applicant waiting area and wandered around the facility at will.

Hattiesburg, Mississippi, is, of course, not typical, but then nowhere really is. It is home to a medium-sized university, the University of Southern Mississippi, which according to the personnel at the MESC operates an active and effective student employment service. This drains university students away from the state office, but there is some student traffic because there are two junior colleges and a small private college nearby. The region's economy is healthy, with low unemployment and fairly high wages, by Mississippi standards anyway. According to the placement supervisor, the standard starting wage before the minimum wage increase of September 1, 1997, was $5.50 per hour. The rise in the minimum wage therefore had no discernible effect, either on the need for employees or the number of applicants. In addition to the university, the community has strong retail and medical sectors as well as several light manufacturing concerns.

Jobs are posted on a large board, with a brief description and a number. There was no shortage of jobs. Applicants register in a book, survey the listings, and write down three selections. Interviewers—there are five general interviewers[12]—call them in the order they register. The interviews are conducted in semiprivate cubicles. The interviewer takes the three job numbers and brings up more information on a computer screen. If the applicant's background, much of which is ascertained verbally, matches the job, the interviewer explains more about the position: the company name, the hours, the promotion possibilities, and so forth. If interested, the applicant is given an introduction card and is told whom to see and the time to appear.

Two things struck me immediately. One was that the office was airier and better kept than I had expected. The carpet and walls were clean and fresh looking. The atmosphere was businesslike but comfortable. The other was that the interviewers treated the applicants with far more respect and sense of dignity than I had thought I would see. Interviewers average 25–30 people a day, and it would be quite easy, it seems to me, to see each one as an interchangeable bureaucratic peg. Also, there is clearly a class gap between the interviewers and most (but by no means all) applicants, the typical interviewer being a college graduate. However, there seemed a genuine sense of concern and level of politeness that I do not think was attributable, entirely anyway, to my presence.

There were usually 15–20 applicants waiting to be interviewed. The racial and gender mix varied throughout the day, but I would guess that it was about 40 percent African American and 60 percent female.[13] There were very few teenagers, and only a handful of people appeared over thirty.

One interesting fact, mentioned by the office manager in our initial conversation and confirmed by the interviews I witnessed, was that many of the applicants were currently employed but looking for something more suitable. He said about 60 percent fit this category; among those whose interviews I attended, the number was 67 percent.

The most common reason employed females gave was a desire to get off a night shift. All those with children said that without calling on relatives, they simply could not get child care at night. One interviewer volunteered during a break that although this had long been something of a concern, it was a growing problem since more women were coming off welfare. Several applicants said they would take lower wages or a harder job if they could work days. For men, the most common reason for wanting a new job was to get more hours. Here, too, some were willing to drop their rate of pay in exchange for a promise of more hours.

One striking fact was how short a time many of the people had been in their current jobs or, for those not presently employed, how short their last period of employment was. The longest I heard was three months, but three to six weeks was much more typical. The MESC personnel confirmed that there is a high turnover rate in most of the low-wage jobs they fill. None of them would hazard a guess when I asked, "How long do you think the average at or near minimum wage worker stays in a minimum wage job, either through getting a raise or leaving?" More than one said simply "not long." They also indicated that there are a certain number of people who are in and out of the work force. They tend to work a while, quit, and then come back in a few months to take another job.

This high turnover throws an interesting light on the percentages given earlier. Those figures may well present an accurate snapshot of the minimum wage work force at a given moment, but it is a constantly moving scene. Another snapshot three months or a year later might give the same statistical portrait, but the people would be different. Or would they? If those who work at or near the minimum wage are moving in and out of the work force and changing jobs regularly, two snapshots separated by, say, six months might capture many of the same faces.

One especially articulate young man, there because there were rumors of layoffs where he worked, left a particularly lasting impression. "When you are paid more," he said, "you are motivated. You are motivated to work and you feel better about yourself. When you get $5.15 an hour you just don't feel worth very much."

5

Policy-Making:
Raising the Minimum Wage in 1996

The minimum wage increase legislated in 1996 was the result of one of those unforeseen and unpredictable quirks of American politics. Several political factors converged to produce what every political observer would have wagered heavily against throughout 1995 and much of the first half of 1996. Not only was Congress controlled by Republicans, but also House Republican leaders and most of the phalanx supporting them were market fundamentalists. Even in the Senate, where the center of political gravity was a bit more moderate, the party's number one and two men—Bob Dole of Kansas and Trent Lott of Mississippi—were known opponents of the minimum wage. Yet, in the end, both houses adopted a law moving the minimum wage up by ninety cents, or 21 percent, precisely what the president had asked for.

Background

Bill Clinton mentioned increasing the minimum wage in his 1992 election campaign, but the idea was promptly shelved after the election.[1] The president decided to concentrate on health care, and many in the administration hoped business backing could be secured for the planned reforms. Any move that might antagonize business interest groups therefore had to be pushed to one side.

Secretary of Labor Robert Reich became the minimum wage's advocate in the administration. In early August of 1993, he sent the president a confidential memo urging him to support an increase. As usual in Washington, it was promptly leaked, this time to the *Wall Street Journal*.[2] A small whirlwind blew for a few days, but nothing came of it. A year later, in September 1994, after the defeat of the health care initiative, Reich tried again, sending a memo suggesting that Clinton signal his "clear intention to raise the minimum wage."[3]

According to Reich, it was on a trip with the president to Illinois in early January of 1995 that he finally convinced Clinton to publicly support a minimum wage increase. In a ride to the airport, Clinton agreed to put it in his upcoming State of the Union address. Others in the administration, including Leon Panetta, the chief of staff, and Robert Rubin, the secretary of the treasury, argued against the move. It would waste too much political capital by embroiling the president in an unwinnable fight, they believed, and at the same time risk making him appear a captive of traditional Democratic interest groups, namely unions.

In the longest State of the Union speech ever, Clinton did include a rather bland reference to raising the minimum wage:

> The goal of building the middle class and shrinking the underclass is also why I believe that you should raise the minimum wage.
>
> It rewards work. . . . In terms of real buying power, by next year, the minimum wage will be at a 40 year low. That's not my idea of how the new economy ought to work.
>
> Now I studied the arguments and the evidence for and against the minimum-wage increase. I believe the weight of the evidence is that a modest increase does not cost jobs and may even lure people back into the market. But the most important thing is you can't make a living on $4.25 an hour. . . .
>
> In the past the minimum wage has been a bipartisan issue and I think it should be again. . . .
>
> Members of Congress have been here less than a month but by the end of the week—28 days into the new year—every member of Congress will have earned as much in congressional salary as a minimum-wage worker makes all year long.[4]

What he omitted was a specific figure for a suggested increase. In the world of politics, many in the press took this as a sign that he was not really serious.

While reporters were asking administration leaders to clarify whether the president was committed to an increase, there was bickering in the White House. Some wanted to spread the word that naming a figure did not matter, since it was not going to pass anyway; others were insisting that a figure had to be released to indicate seriousness. Secretary Reich was scheduled to meet with Democratic congressional leaders on February 2. Before he went, he was instructed by Panetta that the president should not be forced to take the lead on this matter. Sentiment at the meeting was divided, but the consensus was that if a fight was going to be launched, the president would have to "take the lead." In short, everyone knew it would be a bruising, perhaps bloody, battle, and volunteers to carry the battering ram were few.

The following day, partly to still the waters within the administration and among congressional Democrats, Clinton gathered some dignitaries and made a public announcement that he supported a ninety-cent raise. Reich felt Clinton was merely going through the motions, though, since he said it with little evident conviction, "the same way he'd make the case for extending patents on hybrid corn."[5] The battering ram apparently still lay on the ground.

Reluctance among White House insiders and congressional Democrats to lead the charge was not irrational. Republican reaction was swift. Representative Dick Armey of Texas, the House majority leader and a former economics professor, vowed to fight it "with every fiber of my being."[6] House Speaker Newt Gingrich noted simply, "I personally am very skeptical of it, and I think it will kill jobs for minority teenagers." The president of the National Federation of Independent Businesses, an organization that had been instrumental in killing Clinton's health care reform, snarled that it was "a regressive and job-killing scheme which will put a big dent in small-business hiring." Senator Robert Bennett, a Republican from Utah, went further: "The minimum wage should be abolished. If someone isn't worth $4.25 an hour, he should be paid less."[7]

The Joint Economic Committee, chaired by James Saxton, a staunchly conservative member of the House from New Jersey, opened hearings in late February.[8] Although Reich and other supporters were given the opportunity to testify, it was mostly an opportunity for opponents to sound off. In his opening remarks, Saxton displayed two silly graphs showing the "Unanimous View" and the "Reich View" of the relationship between employment and the minimum wage. In the former, a roughly 45° line sloped down—higher minimum wage, lower employment; in the latter, a similar line sloped upward—higher minimum wage, higher employment. "Why then," if Reich is right, "don't we

just raise the minimum wage to $300 or $400 an hour and pay everyone lawyers' wages?" In a calmer moment, Saxton drew the philosophical line: "I believe there is a better way to go. It is called getting
Government out of the process of affecting the process of job creation
and economic growth."[9] Reich felt, apparently rightly, that the issue
was headed for oblivion and that the sole purpose served by Saxton's
antics was keeping it alive. The only other activity in 1995 was a set
of more sober, but almost entirely neglected, hearings by the Senate
Committee on Labor and Human Resources in December.[10]

Moving to the Active Agenda

The proposed minimum wage increase got a hand from an unlikely
source, Pat Buchanan's Republican primary campaign for the presidency. Buchanan acidly attacked the problems of job insecurity and
falling real wages for American workers during what seemed to be
good economic times. Although his solutions did not include a minimum wage boost, his upstart victory in New Hampshire put stagnant
wages and economic anxieties in the newspapers. In time, Bob Dole
subdued Buchanan, but the issue did not go away. Back in Washington, election-year politicking, coupled with the arcane rules of the
Senate, soon gave minimum wage advocates a golden opening.

   As Dole sewed up his party's presidential nomination, he faced a
strategic choice. Should he give up his post as Senate majority leader
or perhaps even his Senate seat itself and concentrate full-time on the
fall campaign? Or should he remain? Feeling his command of the Senate would enable him to push legislation through, some of which he
apparently hoped Clinton would veto, he elected to stay and try to
fashion an image as a man of accomplishment. If successful, he believed
the contrast with the president would provide an inherent political
advantage.

   The rules of the Senate are legendary both for their oddity and their
complexity.[11] The oddest is the filibuster, which allows senators to talk
as long as they wish on any subject whatever.[12] In effect, this tactic grinds
the Senate to a halt. A filibuster can be broken only by sixty senators
voting to close off debate and have a vote on the bill under consider-

ation. If you have 41 votes, you can stop any bill and all other pending legislation. At one time, filibusters were used sparingly. In the last decade or so, though, they have become much more common. For most controversial legislation, it usually takes 60 votes these days to secure passage. In 1996, the party split in the Senate was 53 Republicans and 47 Democrats, which should have been a warning sign to Dole.

At the same time, there are many complex rules about what types of amendments can be offered to what bills under what circumstances. If a majority leader is determined enough, knowledgeable enough, and wily enough, he can usually block amendments on subjects he dislikes. It takes great effort and carries substantial risks, but it can be done.

Senator Ted Kennedy of Massachusetts had been steadfastly pushing the minimum wage hike since the president's State of the Union speech. He had appeared before committees, made speeches, and pushed the administration to devote more energy to the cause. With public backing running about four to one in favor of a minimum wage increase, as shown in the polls discussed in chapter 3, Kennedy convinced the Senate minority leader, Tom Daschle of South Dakota, that they had an ideal opportunity to secure the measure's passage or, if not, inject some discomfort into the Republican presidential campaign.

Center Stage

On March 26, the day Dole wrapped up the nomination by winning the California primary, Senate Democrats took advantage of an obscure parliamentary maneuver and introduced the ninety-cent minimum wage increase as an amendment to an innocuous bill the body was considering. By all accounts, Dole was completely blindsided. He scrambled and dug into the labyrinthine rulebook to locate a parliamentary move to check a vote that day. As he left the chamber, he was heard to mutter, "That won't happen again."[13] Kennedy told reporters, "The day Bob Dole locks up the Republican nomination, he locks out American families who are looking for a very modest increase."[14] Asked whether he and Daschle had done it purposely on this particular day, Kennedy replied, "We haven't lost any sleep over it." Dole retorted, "I assume that sooner or later the issue will be debated and voted on, directly or indirectly, but not today, not tomorrow, and not next week."[15]

Though Dole had blocked the vote on March 26, the item was still officially on the agenda. He now had to call for a filibuster, since four Republican moderates had indicated they favored the minimum wage bill.[16] This would have given the proponents the 51 votes they needed for passage. With a filibuster, though, they had to get 60. On March 28, they mustered only 55.[17] Daschle, however, promised, "We will be back offering this week after week, until we get it passed."[18]

Other Democrats now took Kennedy's and Daschle's cue. Clinton renewed his call for a minimum wage increase in his next Saturday's radio address. House minority leader Dick Gephardt next tried to get the House to schedule a vote on the issue. A motion on a vote to have a vote failed twice, 232-180 and 226-192. Like Daschle, Gephardt promised to keep the issue alive.[19]

It was the Senate, though, that became the focus of action. Every time a bill came to the floor—on immigration, paying the legal expenses of fired White House travel personnel, or whatever—the Democrats offered their minimum wage amendment. This forced Dole to use his parliamentary powers to prevent a vote on the amendment, but when he did not allow the amendment, the Democrats would filibuster the main bill. Because he did not have 60 votes, he could not break the logjam. The Senate ground to a halt as every day became minimum wage day.

Interest groups swung into action. The AFL-CIO launched a campaign called "America Needs a Raise." It aired television and radio spots in states and districts of moderate or vulnerable Republican members of Congress. On April 16, thirteen Republicans in the House, most from the Northeast and Midwest, announced they favored the minimum wage increase. This still did not give the hike's backers a majority in the House, even if every Democrat and the one independent all voted yes. However, it was a significant crack in the Republican wall. Meanwhile, business groups geared up a large-scale lobbying campaign of their own.

From a purely political perspective, nothing could be going better for the Democrats, or worse for Dole. He was on the wrong side of a popular issue; he appeared to be stifling democracy by not even allowing a vote; he was tied down in the Senate; he was caught between moderate and pragmatic Republicans who wanted to vote and put the issue behind them and the die-hard conservatives and business interests who were adamantly opposed to doing so; and his reputation for legislative effectiveness was being tarnished. One Democratic strategist gloated, "Every day spent on the minimum wage is another good day for the Democrats."[20]

On April 17, seven more House Republicans defected, making the count twenty altogether. Gingrich reluctantly told the GOP caucus the same day that Republicans might as well begin preparing for a vote.

During the next two weeks, the Democrats continued their full court press of publicity and ridicule. Representative David Bonior from Michigan weighed in with the observation, "The strategy of the Republican leadership sounds like the name of a Washington law firm: duck it, block it, bury it, and delay."[21] Representative Pat Williams from Montana trusted many people had read Dickens (or seen the movie) as he lifted an empty bowl toward the Capitol ceiling and intoned, "Please, sir, may I have more?"[22] Meanwhile, they continually tried to force a vote in both chambers, each time unsuccessfully.

Stalled Counterattack

Publicly, the Republicans were in disarray and fighting among themselves. Dick Armey called the Democrats' moves "a sham on the part of the Washington union bosses that fund the Democratic Party."[23] Moderates, especially those from areas with strong unions, thought Armey and Gingrich were overdoing the union bashing. Representative Peter King, a Republican from New York, told *Newsday,* "It's a southern, anti-union attitude that appeals to the mentality of hillbillies at revival meetings."[24] Gingrich and Armey offered up a half-baked plan to increase the Earned Income Tax Credit and other items, but it was pulled almost as quickly. The chief lobbyist for the National Federation of Independent Businesses delivered a coded threat: "A lot of our members are shaking their heads at the prospect of a Republican Congress passing this. They say 'Tell me again who's doing this to us. Aren't these our friends? Aren't they the ones we made a majority?'"[25]

Behind the scenes, though, Gingrich and Dole were working on the old standby strategy for these situations, the rider. If a minimum wage had to be voted on, they would seek to add other items to it. If enough moderate Republicans could be convinced to support these, something which seemed likely, the onus would then be on congressional Democrats and the president. It would force them to approve the minimum wage along with something they disliked or, alternately, compel them to oppose the minimum wage increase. Either way, the Democrats, not the Republicans, would then be on the political hot seat. Of course, this strategy could backfire, if the president and his allies in Congress could convince the public that the rider itself was holding up action.[26]

There were four different measures that stood out as candidates for such a move. The first was repeal of the 4.3 cent a gallon gasoline tax, which Dole had been trying to sell on the campaign trail. A second was a package of small business tax cuts and incentives. The problem was that the Democrats would probably accept both, especially to get the minimum wage. Two other issues favored by many Republicans were anathema to the unions and to most Democrats, however. The first of these was the so-called compensatory time proposal. The Fair Labor Standards Act requires payment of overtime at one-and-a-half times the regular hourly rate for any hours worked over forty per week. Republicans argued that the rule was designed for the industrial conditions of the 1930s and was ill-suited to contemporary conditions. They wanted to allow employees to take time off later for overtime instead of being paid for it. Unions strongly opposed this idea because they feared employers would demand that workers choose time off rather than receive pay. The other was what is referred to as the "TEAM" proposal. Under it, employers could set up committees of workers to deal with workplace issues. Unions saw this as opening the door to the "company unions" that proliferated in the 1920s. If either of these was added to the minimum wage bill, Dole and Gingrich thought, unions would probably sacrifice the minimum wage to keep them off the statute books. But if not, Republicans would have secured one of their legislative goals.

The president's people notified Congress that adding either the compensatory time proposal or the TEAM law would be considered a "poison pill," prompting a certain veto. Moderate Republicans pressured their leaders not to force a showdown with the president by including them, fearing that it would merely give Clinton more political advantage.

Action in the House of Representatives

While Senate Democrats kept Dole dancing to their tune in the Senate, pressure was building in the House to have a vote. Each time the Democrats managed to force a procedural vote on whether to have a vote, a few more Republicans deserted the leadership. Hoping to salvage what they could, Gingrich and his lieutenants offered the Democrats a package of small business tax cuts in exchange for a vote on the minimum wage, which everyone now believed was certain to pass. Democratic leaders agreed, and the Ways and Means Committee cobbled together a $7 billion assortment of such measures. At the insistence of conservative hardliners, it was agreed that the two bills would be voted on separately, so that they would not have to vote for any bill containing a minimum wage increase. May 23 was set for the day of the vote.

Until midday May 21, all appeared set. Then Representative William Goodling, a Republican from Pennsylvania who was chair of the Committee on Education and the Workforce, let it be known that he intended to introduce three amendments to the minimum wage bill,[27] all of which were controversial. Only one, however, seemed capable of derailing the agreement. The first was to reinstate the "training wage" that had consumed so much energy in 1989. It was adopted then but had expired in 1993. Goodling's proposal was to allow firms to pay $4.25 an hour to anyone under twenty for their first ninety days of employment. Although Democrats generally opposed a subminimum wage of any kind, their ardor was cooled by the fact that when it had been in effect from 1990 to 1993, it was very seldom used.[28] The second involved how the "tip credit" was calculated. Under then existing law, businesses had to pay all tipped workers at least 50 percent of the minimum wage whatever their tips totaled. Goodling's plan was to freeze the required payment at $2.13, with the proviso that the employer would have to make up the difference if the employee did not reach the minimum wage. In essence, most tipped employees would not receive a raise. Again, most Democrats did not like this idea, but it was not serious enough to lose the general increase over.

The third proposal, however, posed a more serious threat. Recall (chapter 2) that in 1989 the small business exemption had been set at $500,000 for all types of enterprises. Congress had also tampered with the underlying definition of who was covered by the Fair Labor Standards Act that year though. The Department of Labor had subsequently issued a regulation based on the new wording that made any employee who dealt in any way with interstate commerce subject to the act, no matter what the size of the company. Since it is rare to find someone whose work does not in some fashion touch interstate commerce—handling goods from out of state, answering long-distance phone calls, etc.—it virtually erased the exemption. Goodling now proposed to reinstate and legally insulate a blanket exemption for all businesses grossing under $500,000 annually.

Sensing its importance, the Rules Committee scheduled a vote on this issue apart from the other two items.[29] No one was sure whether enough moderate Republicans and conservative Democrats would vote for it to secure its adoption. (This is unusual on the House floor, as the outcome is ordinarily known well in advance.) Democrats pleaded that it would exempt two-thirds of all businesses in the United States and remove 10.5 million workers from minimum wage coverage. It would also, they said, lead to the reinstitution of sweatshops, since many companies would find ways to set up mini-subcontractors. While accurate, both these contentions were misleading. Small "mom and pop" firms may make up two-thirds of business enterprises, but they account for only a small fraction of the nation's commerce. On the second matter, no one knew how many of the 10.5 million employees working at these concerns made the minimum wage. Moreover, economists doubted such an exemption would have much real effect, since the minimum wage tends to become a general scale everyone uses in low-wage labor markets.[30] It was the measure's symbolism that was really most troubling to Democrats. It would make the Fair Labor

Standards Act less than universal, and that opened the way to other possible gaps in the future. Clinton, for his part, threatened to veto the bill if the amendment carried. In the end, the margin of defeat was much larger than anyone expected, 229-196. The other two installments of what the Democrats labeled "Goodling's surprise" were approved, however.

After an impassioned debate, the House adopted the main bill easily, 281-144, 187 Democrats and 93 Republicans making up the majority.

The House Debate

The debate that occurred in the House over the Goodling amendments and the main bill can be examined with some profit. It is not that debates in Congress ever change anyone's mind, inside or outside the body. However, they reveal something of a composite picture of what public figures think the important arguments are concerning the legislation at hand.[31]

Supporters of the minimum wage hike stressed repeatedly that the minimum wage was near a forty-year low in purchasing power and that the 1991 increase (voted on in 1989) had been overtaken by inflation. The ninety-cent raise would therefore simply return its value to the 1991 level. It was never spelled out, though, why either of these should be the standard for measuring the minimum wage. The implication, of course, was that it was not too high in 1955 (the year used for comparison) or 1991, but this was purely a subjective judgment.

More telling was comparing the minimum wage with the poverty level. It was noted constantly that a full-time minimum wage worker made $170 per week, or $8,500 a year.[32] The official poverty level for a family of three stood at $12,980 and for a family of four, $15,600. They bolstered the relevancy of these figures by alluding to the demographics of the minimum wage work force: the percentage who were adults (repeated over and over to answer charges that the raise helped mostly teenagers), the number who worked full-time, and the percentage who were women. An often cited figure (provided by Reich) was that the "average" minimum wage worker contributed half of family income.

While this is a much more realistic scaling device for establishing the level of the minimum wage, it has its own problems. Is the poverty line what we desire for someone who works full-time? Is this the limit of what a public policy that extols work can do? Since few people remain at the minimum wage if they stay employed any length of time, is the poverty threshold even relevant? Should we expect one worker on one job to support a family of three or four? No one said it, but if the modern norm is or should be two working adults in a household, then a husband and wife could earn $17,000 together (and have two weeks vacation), which would lift a family of three out of poverty. If one of them worked another eight hours at a second job, something many people do, especially as they establish a toehold in the work force, their income would climb to $18,700 (or $19,448 if they did not take or were paid for a vacation). This is not a middle-class income, to be sure, but it is above the official poverty line.

There were plenty of platitudes offered about the value of work, that it is uplifting, socially valuable, and so forth. While undoubtedly often sincerely meant, it sounded somewhat hollow coming from many who had been less than eager through the years to establish meaningful work requirements in the nation's welfare program. More pointed were their allusions to the current spate of attempted welfare reforms. If we seriously expected people who have been on welfare to work rather than stay on public assistance, we should make sure that the jobs they get pay a decent wage.

The Republican offensive on the minimum wage's purported negative employment effects was countered chiefly by referring to the work of Princeton University economists David Card and Alan Krueger (to be discussed later).[33] They found that employment actually went up in New Jersey when it raised its state minimum wage. Other studies were marshaled to show that even if there were disemployment effects, they were trivial.

Occasionally, however, the idea of fundamental fairness and basic human dignity surfaced. Christopher Shays, a Republican from Connecticut, said, "In my heart I believe that we have got to have a minimum base for a worker so they are not exploited. In my heart I believe this is the right thing to do." Richard Gephardt added, "Are we going to say that somebody that carries a bedpan in a hospital, cleaning up the people in the hospital, is not worth anything?" Finally, there was Albert Wynn of Maryland, who declared, "This debate is about the American dream. This debate is about standards of living in America."

Other than castigating the policy in general (as "a charlatan game" and a "sham"), opponents largely confined themselves to two themes: the potential for job losses, particularly for minorities and the poor; and its interference with the market's smooth operation. A few references were made to the possible inflationary effects and a rise in business failures, but these were secondary.

Mark Souder, a Republican from Indiana, told his colleagues, "I understand it is called a minimum wage bill, but in fact it is a layoff bill. . . . Kids will lose their jobs, minorities will lose their jobs, senior citizens will lose their jobs. In small towns, in center cities, marginal businesses will be devastated." Tim Hutchinson, an Arkansas Republican, added, "We know that raising the minimum wage is a job killer on the most vulnerable people in our society." John Shadegg, a Republican from Arizona, claimed that one of every four minority workers between seventeen and twenty-four would be out of work:[34] "This is an unemployment act that hurts minority youth, and that is a shame." Texas Republican Tom DeLay won the cute barb of the day award: "The Democrat Party is to job creation what Dr. Kevorkian is to health care, a job-killer cloaked in kindness."

The literature on the minimum wage's employment effects will be analyzed momentarily. What is interesting politically is who is making these arguments. It is simply hard to take seriously their claims that they stayed up nights worrying about minority youths. In no other area of public policy did they evidence much concern for these people, and minorities were certainly not part of the Republican voting constituency. It would be too cynical, perhaps, to say that it was purely a political shell game when they called up these arguments, but they did stretch credulity quite far. More plausible was their concern for inflation and business failures, two more traditional Republican songs. Did this overwhelming focus on possible job losses, though, particularly job losses among minority teens, say something about their view of the American public philosophy and, in turn, something about that philosophy? That is, if they did not believe many people care about the fate of minority teens, would they have expended so much effort making the argument?

The philosophical position was stated most directly and candidly by George Radanovich, a Republican from California: "In the private sector, the minimum wage is an interference with employer-employee contractual relations. Big brothers in the Federal bureaucracy aren't happy unless they can control conduct throughout the workplace."

Final Approval

Dole resigned from the Senate to run for president as a private citizen on May 15. Republicans elevated Trent Lott of Mississippi to the majority leader's post and selected Don Nickles of Oklahoma as their whip. The political chemistry was thus altered. Lott was even more strongly opposed to the minimum wage than Dole was, and Nickles was a firebrand on the issue. Moreover, neither of them was under the kind of election-year pressure that surrounded Dole. Polls therefore had less immediacy in their minds, although Lott was not unmindful of the effect this battle could have on the congressional elections overall. Further, none of the eight Republican moderates in the Senate who had voted with the Democrats on March 28 was up for reelection. They were therefore not as prone as their House counterparts to succumb to union blandishments. Nonetheless, Lott was known for his ability to find compromises and move legislation forward.

Democrats called off their "amendment to every bill" tactic during June. This session of Congress was drawing to a close, and Daschle was becoming pessimistic that he could force a vote. On June 11, however, he threatened to renew the guerrilla tactics if Lott made no concessions toward naming a date for a vote. After days of delicate negotiations, the two party leaders managed to forge a plan acceptable to both. The Senate Finance Committee would draft a tax cut bill, starting with the House-approved version. It would then be combined with the minimum wage bill passed by the House. On the floor, each side could offer one amendment to the minimum wage portion of the bill. The Democratic version was to be written by Senator Kennedy and the Republican one developed by Christopher Bond from Missouri, chair of the Senate's Small Business Committee. After the votes were recorded on these two amendments, individual senators could offer amendments to the tax part of the bill. The vote would then be up or down on the entire package. After that, the Senate would take up the TEAM bill on a separate vote.

The real struggle centered on the two amendments. Bond put three items into his: (1) the $500,000 small business exemption voted down in the House; (2) the lengthening of the training wage to 180 days and removal of the age stipulation; and (3) a delay in the effective date of the law. Kennedy had two items relating to the minimum wage, along with a proposal on hours.[35] The two minimum wage matters were (1) shortening the training wage period to 30 days; and (2) reinstating the 50 percent tip credit provision.

Interest groups and the administration stepped up their already intense lobbying efforts. The AFL-CIO, which had spent $2.6 million to date, took out more ads, set up phone banks, and urged its locals to contact their senators, particularly the fence sitters. The National Retail Federation's John Motley called on his members to flood the Senate with calls and faxes in support of the Bond amendment. "It is," he told them, "our last chance and best hope for stopping the minimum wage increase this year." He felt certain that Democrats would scuttle the bill rather than see it included. Reich and administration aides wandered the halls of the Capitol all during the day of the vote. Vice President Gore took over the presiding chair in the Senate, in case there was a tie. Emboldened by the turn of events, the White House threatened to veto the measure if any of the three sections of the Bond amendment was successful.

In the end, the Bond amendment failed 52-46, as five Republicans joined with all the Democrats, even though two of the Democrats had earlier expressed support for the small business exemption. When it came time for Kennedy's proposal, the people were different but the arithmetic identical, a 52-46 loss. That behind them, senators turned to the more agreeable task of offering a variety of amendments to the tax section of the bill, which swelled to a $19 billion cut for large and small businesses as well as a range of special interest groups.[36] The master bill then glided to an easy 74-24 victory. A final hurdle seemed to be thrown up when Nickles threatened to block the appointment of conferees in retaliation for Kennedy's similar tactic on a Republican-sponsored health care plan.

Both men soon relented, however, and the bill headed to conference. Since the minimum wage half of the measure was identical in both House and Senate versions, attention focused on the tax cuts, the details of which were speedily ironed out.

On August 20, President Clinton held a ceremony on the South Lawn of the White House to sign the bill. Labor leaders, the vice president, Democratic and Republican backers of the bill, and a swarm of children of minimum wage workers were all present. It was perfect theater, and pundits duly noted that the president was utilizing it apparently to gather momentum for the upcoming Democratic convention. At the convention, however, the president gave a speech detailing the accomplishments of his first administration and did not even mention the minimum wage hike. Although it had generated more political heat and consumed more hours of strategic planning than any other matter at the most recent congressional session, it now quietly disappeared once again from the political world. Nevertheless, 10–11 million Americans did get a raise on October 1, 1996, and another one on September 1, 1997.

Patterns of Policy-Making

At the broadest level of generalization, policy-making follows the model laid out in figure 4.[37] Problems move onto the political agenda; political decisions are taken; implementation, usually by an executive agency, follows; and then evaluation and feedback take place, leading to new demands.

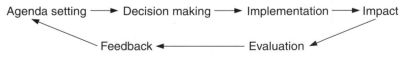

Figure 4. General Model of Policy-Making

The decision-making stage in the 1996 minimum wage increase followed a rather simple pattern. A group of committed proponents was arrayed against a group of committed opponents. Interest groups lined up on one side or the other. A band of moderates sat in the middle, holding the fate of the bill in their hands. The opponents tried the standard tactic of amending the bill to dilute it (e.g., to delay the effective date, to nibble at who could be given the raise) and make the bill more palatable to their tastes (e.g., the small business tax cuts). They even tried to sabotage it entirely by attaching amendments so distasteful to the bill's backers (e.g., the Goodling and Bond amendments) that they would abandon it. As opponents proposed each amendment, they hoped to draw a few moderates to their cause. The outcome of the intricate game of move and countermove was not certain until the defeat of the Bond amendment in the Senate. For all the complexity of the tactics, this was a straightforward, almost textbook example of how legislation is passed.[38]

As the brief sketches in chapter 2 indicate and more detailed studies confirm,[39] this pattern has been replicated each time the minimum wage has been increased. But the decision-making stage can begin only when the issue works its way onto the serious political agenda. How does this vital link in the chain of policy-making occur? How does a proposal to boost the minimum wage move from obscurity to become the issue of the day?

Political scientists have been studying agendas since the publication of Roger Cobb and Charles Elder's path-breaking book in 1972.[40] A general model of agenda setting is depicted in figure 5. The usual sequence is for a social problem to occur first, giving rise to demands that government do something to alleviate the situation. Naturally, there is a struggle over how to define the issue, because that will play a large part in determining the plans that are considered and ultimately adopted, if any action is taken at all. Slowly, an issue moves onto the

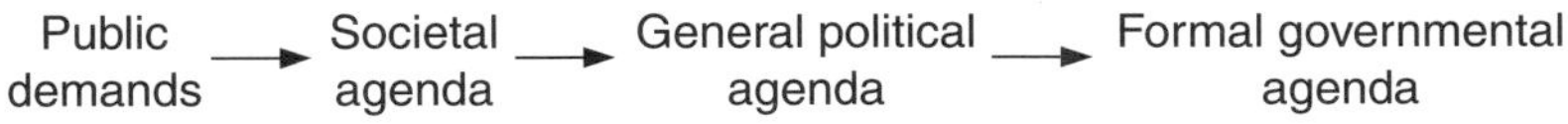

Public demands → Societal agenda → General political agenda → Formal governmental agenda

Figure 5. Usual Agenda-Setting Model

general governmental agenda, usually through interest groups pressing demands or the actions of political parties. Next, the formal governmental agenda—the calendars of legislative bodies, dockets of
courts, a list of possible executive orders—is penetrated. Then, the age-
old pull and tug of politics shapes the final action.

The minimum wage increase, however, did not work this way.[41] As
we saw in chapter 3, the public's feelings about a minimum wage boost
were more passive than active. The issue simply did not register until
politicians and the press began talking about it. Not just any politi-
cian pushing a minimum wage hike can get the public's attention,
however. Moreover, the issue must become explicitly visible. It seems
that minimum wage increases, in 1996 as well as in previous years,
came onto the agenda as sketched out in figure 6.

Bills to increase the minimum wage are introduced in virtually every congressional session.[42] Moreover, if the administration is Democratic, there is ordinarily someone in the White House circle who thinks
raising the minimum wage is a sound idea. The issue is therefore always put on the formal agenda of Congress and often on the president's
desk as well. In 1996, both Robert Reich and Senator Ted Kennedy
played the role of what could be labeled "instigator." Reich wrote
memos and verbally pushed the idea to the president. Kennedy introduced legislation and talked it up incessantly. As is customary, the
proposal was going nowhere.

The crucial stage occurs when the instigators convince other politicians who have more visibility than they do to adopt the idea. Let us
call these people "enablers." In 1996, it was when Bill Clinton and
Tom Daschle took up the cause that the proposal became a serious
political matter. Daschle's support was far more important than
Clinton's in this case. Of course, the political calculations surrounding the 1996 presidential election obviously figured heavily in Daschle's

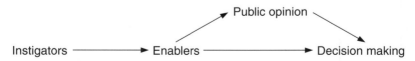

Figure 6. Minimum Wage Agenda Setting

and Clinton's thinking, but in all of the other years, there were political forces at work also. That political strategy motivated the enablers in 1996 was hardly unique. The general point is that for some reason, politicians with power to shape the political debate scoop the minimum wage increase off the formal agenda and move it onto the serious political agenda.

At this point, the public becomes aware that a minimum wage increase is under discussion. Invariably, it endorses the idea by a substantial margin, giving the proponents important political ammunition. Because of its low saliency, though, public opinion on the issue does not enter into the political fray directly. Nonetheless, it is a potent background factor, and there may be politically vulnerable members—as in 1996—who find it convenient to swim with the tide. Or it may influence party leaders in one way or another. To cite one example of party leaders' use of public opinion, when Democrats became convinced in 1989 that public backing was not strong enough to embarrass Bush after his veto, they brought more compromises to the table.

In short, the fact that a minimum wage increase receives the endorsement of well-known politicians does not guarantee that it will pass. The legislative battle must still be won. In 1987, for instance, the issue won a place on the political agenda but was voted down. Winning the support of the enablers is a necessary but hardly sufficient condition for getting the increase actually adopted.

To return to the general model of figure 4, once the law is on the statute books and goes into effect (via the Department of Labor's enforcement program), the evaluation of the policy's impact and the feedback stage begin. It is to those that we turn in the following chapter.

6
Impact and Feedback

Even though the politics of the minimum wage is largely symbolic, it still has tangible impact as an economic regulatory policy. As depicted in the model sketched out in the preceding chapter, in the usual course of events, the effects of public policies produce feedback to the decision makers in government. The feedback leads, in turn, to modification or perhaps termination of the policy.

There are ordinarily three channels by which the impact of public policies is communicated to those in power. The first is government-mandated studies and analyses. Congress habitually orders executive agencies to monitor the effects of the laws it enacts and to relay that information back. Environmental, educational, and tax policies, for instance, are subject to continual analysis by the agencies charged with their execution. These findings are regularly transmitted to Congress by a series of reports and publications and often through congressional hearings as well. Normally, of course, members of Congress do not spend much time poring over these items; instead, staff people glean them for what they think relevant and pass that on to the member. At times, however, an evaluative report will stir media attention and thereby force itself into congressional consciousness.

The Department of Labor has conducted and published any number of analyses of how the minimum wage is working. The annual reports of the secretary of labor are replete with data and information. The journal *Monthly Labor Review,* published by the Department of Labor, has a plethora of articles dealing with the minimum wage. Further, special economic studies of the minimum wage were ordered by Congress when it raised the minimum wage in 1955, 1961, and 1966.[1] None of them, however, sparked the slightest interest in Congress or the news media when they were completed. In 1977, Congress created the Minimum Wage Study Commission at the same time it raised the minimum wage. Its purpose was to conduct the most far-ranging and comprehensive analyses done to date on every aspect of the minimum wage. Prominent economists were engaged, and an enormous amount of material was finally published in 1981.[2] By then, the Reagan administration had taken office, and only apathy greeted the release of these volumes. While the commission's labors have been an important source of information for scholars through the years, they have had no impact whatsoever on policy-making.

Another common feedback mechanism is interest groups. Alive to how public policies are affecting their members or their area of concern (such as the environment), they are quick to inform friendly members of Congress of what is happening. Of course, such pleading is sharply biased, but many in Congress often say that such contacts provide invaluable information. According to most accounts, members of Congress rely heavily on this flow of ideas and information.[3]

There is, however, no National Association of Minimum Wage Workers. These citizens have no Washington lobbyists to call in or fax to congressional offices the latest movements in employment and prices that relate to their welfare. They have no organization to generate letter-writing campaigns and hold no conventions to which senators and representatives may be invited to speak—and schmooze. And, of course, they have no political action committee to make campaign contributions to secure the coveted "access."[4] The interest groups that are active in minimum wage politics take up the cause only when it moves onto center stage. For the rest of the time, their energies are focused on other matters. Unions, the most stalwart backers of raising the minimum wage, have a multitude of concerns, concerns that affect the lives of their members far more directly than minimum wage hikes do. While unions can usually be counted on to flex their political muscle when the fight actually begins, they do not communicate the problems of minimum wage workers to members of Congress. Likewise, the constellation of civil rights and women's groups that customarily join unions in supporting minimum wage increases expend their energies elsewhere after the vote is held. Business groups also seem to lose interest after the fight is over. As is shown later, the minimum wage appears to have little measurable effect on economic activity and none on business profits. For all their vocal opposition to it when it is under consideration, business groups therefore do not spend their time complaining about it when it is off the active political agenda. Most of the time, it goes largely unnoticed in the business world.

Finally, politicians receive news of the effects of policies through the ballot box. If schools are inferior, if streets are unsafe, if taxes are too high, or if air pollution is choking a city, people running for office will hear from those affected. This is how a democracy functions. However, the two groups most affected by the minimum wage—the young and the poor—have the lowest rates of voting turnout of any two groups in our society. In the 1994 congressional elections, for example, only 17 percent of those aged 18 to 20 voted, and of course 16- and 17-year-olds were not even eligible. This compares with a 45 percent voter turnout in the overall population. The turnout for those who did not complete high school, which could be used as a surrogate for poverty, was 25 percent.[5] Small wonder that the issues of everyday life confronting minimum wage workers are seldom addressed in a political campaign, unless the issue already happens to be on the agenda.

In short, none of the usual channels of political communication feeds data, information, and arguments back to Congress on how minimum wage workers and their employers are faring. One group of people, however, have long been interested in the minimum wage and its effects: professional economists. According to one tabulation, more articles have been published in economics journals on the minimum wage than on any other federal policy save unemployment insurance.[6] From the perspective of political feedback, however, these studies are done in a void. Whatever their findings, they have no immediate impact on congressional or presidential politics. When the minimum wage moves onto the active agenda, economists are quickly drafted by both sides. They are hustled before congressional committees, and the results of their analyses pepper speeches and press releases. Their work is therefore quite relevant politically, but not in the agenda-setting sense, as it would be if it were part of a continuous feedback process. Instead, economists have episodic influence that occurs only after others manage to put a minimum wage increase on the serious political agenda.

Because of economists' insatiable interest in the minimum wage, we have a rich body of literature on the policy's impact. Extensive analyses have been undertaken, particularly of how the minimum wage affects employment, but its possible role in inflation, business failures, and the reduction of poverty has not been ignored. The problem for the disinterested observer, policymaker, or citizen is that there is little consensus on any of these fronts. Those imbued with an ideology can therefore always find an economist to support their positions. As Sar Levitan and Richard Belous said nearly twenty years ago, "Clearly, econometric results, like Holy Scripture, can be cited by believers of different persuasions."[7]

Employment Effects

In 1909, the British Board of Trade imposed a minimum wage on the chain-making industry. One of the century's most creative economists, R. H. Tawney, was commissioned to analyze the effect of the move. In his introductory remarks, Tawney sounded an optimistic note: "[O]wing to recent departures in legislation evidence is now coming to light which can be used as a partial criterion of the social and economic effects produced by the intervention of a public body to fix minimum rates, and it is therefore possible to appeal, for a solution of certain primary problems, to the light of experience."[8]

The employment effects of minimum wage legislation so fascinate economists largely because it offers a cogent example of a governmental attempt to interfere with a "market." In standard economic theory, demand curves slope down when plotted on price (here wages) and quantity (here the level of employment) axes (see figure 7). That is to say, the higher the price of a commodity, the less will be purchased. Supply curves, in contrast, slope upward. The higher the price of an item, the more will be supplied. Where the two lines intersect is the equilibrium price, the point at which both factors are in balance.

Applied to labor markets, the demand curve represents firms wishing to hire workers, and the supply curve depicts people willing to work for a given wage (the price of labor).[9] The model assumes a large number of firms and no collusion among them. It also assumes that work-

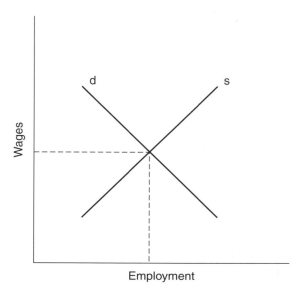

Figure 7. The Conventional Model of Supply and Demand for Labor in the Economy as a Whole (Aggregate Supply and Demand)

ers are interchangeable and that they are not organized; thus, each wage bargain is an individual one.[10] In such a case, firms will have to bid against one another for workers, and workers will have to compete against one another for the jobs. If one employer raises wages, more workers will apply, making for a job queue, and the employer can start offering less and less, until all the slots are filled. Conversely, if an employer offers less than the equilibrium wage, there will be no applicants.

The situation depicted in figure 7 is what happens in the economy as a whole. As for what determines the demand for workers at each firm, an employer seeking to maximize profits will keep adding workers as long as their contribution to revenue exceeds their wage. Since the wage was set by the interaction of aggregate demand and aggregate supply, an infinite number of workers will be available to any one firm (see figure 8).

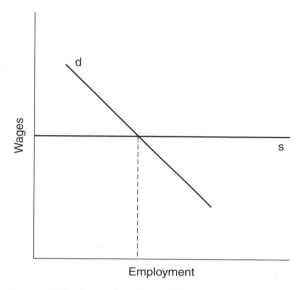

Figure 8. The Conventional Model of Supply and Demand for Labor for Any One Firm

Now, suppose the government enacts a minimum wage at W2,[11] as in the two graphs in figure 9. The price for labor has been forced to an artificial point, above where the demand and supply factors have set the price. Thus, fewer workers (represented by E2 on both graphs) can be hired than were before the minimum wage took effect. The number of workers represented by E1 minus E2 is how many people will lose their jobs in the economy as a whole and at a given firm. The tradeoff is that a certain number are more highly paid, but then others have nothing.[12] Finis Welch put it this way: "In its simplest form a minimum wage law is nothing more than a statement to workers that unless they can find jobs at or above the specified minimum they cannot work."[13]

The model makes intuitive sense. If I am running a profitable business with a hundred workers earning $4.00 per hour each, I have probably hired workers up to the point that additional workers would not

The Economy as a Whole

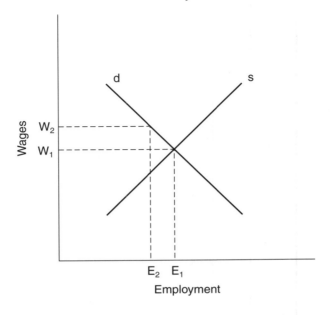

Individual Firm

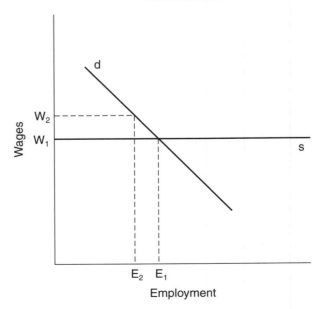

Figure 9. Effects of a Minimum Wage in the Conventional Model

pay their way.[14] The hundredth worker may be generating only $4.05 in revenue for me. I keep the worker employed because it pays me to do so. If a minimum wage of $5.00 per hour is imposed, I will immediately lay off all those who are contributing less than $5.00 per hour to my income statement. Presumably, all firms are affected the same way, and unemployment goes up.

In the real world, though, Tawney found that little, if any, worker displacement took place in the chain-making trade and later in the clothing industry when minimum wages were adopted.[15] In musing about why his findings seemed to run counter to what economic theory said, he penned a conclusion that is as apt today as then: "The ingenuity of employers and workpeople so greatly exceeds that of economists that discussions of what 'must' happen, unsupported by evidence as to what has happened or is happening, are usually quite worthless."[16] In other words, if our goal is to explain reality, perhaps we should consult the data before building a model.

The next series of studies, using the same methods as Tawney, who went out and examined actual businesses and workers, tended to confirm his findings. Richard Lester's study of cotton mills in the 1940s showed that increased minimum wages had no significant impact on employment.[17]

It fell to George Stigler, a future president of the American Economics Association, to put the case for the model over the data. Stigler argued in 1946 that unemployment resulted from minimum wage legislation and that it could not be otherwise: "Whatever the numbers (which no one knows), the direct unemployment is substantial and certain; and it fairly establishes the presumption that the net effects of the minimum wage on aggregate employment are adverse."[18]

The simplest way to test Stigler's broadside is to examine unemployment rates before and after minimum wages go up. As can be seen in table 16, unemployment goes down after minimum wage increases just as often as it goes up. As of 1997, the score is tied at 8 to 8. The major criticism of this approach, of course, is that it does not control for other factors. Believers in the standard model point out (rightly) that growth in the demand for labor could have resulted from general economic growth. Conversely, of course, the rise in unemployment in 1980

The Politics of the Minimum Wage

Table 16. Minimum Wage Increases and the Unemployment Rate

Year	Unemployment Rate in Year Preceding Increase	Unemployment Rate in Year of Increase
1950	5.9%	5.3%
1956	4.4	4.1
1961	5.5	6.7
1963	5.5	5.7
1967	3.8	3.8
1968	3.8	3.6
1974	4.9	5.6
1975	5.6	8.5
1976	8.5	7.7
1978	7.1	6.1
1979	6.1	5.8
1980	5.8	7.1
1981	7.1	7.6
1990	5.3	5.5
1991	5.5	6.7
1996	5.8	5.4
1997	5.4	4.9

Source: Department of Labor, Bureau of Labor Statistics, *Employment and Earnings.*

and 1991 could have been, and surely was, traceable to other causes.[19] If so, the correct comparison is not the unemployment rates before and after minimum wage increases but instead the unemployment rate after a minimum wage increase and what it would have been had there been no minimum wage. Figure 10 presents this argument graphically. Even though unemployment has fallen, the minimum wage is still causing unemployment, since the rate is higher than it would have been otherwise.

There are two possible rejoinders to this criticism. One is that as we have more cases to report (that is, more historical increases in the minimum wage), the odds grow that the other economic factors cancel each other out.[20] This is especially germane because the result is roughly balanced. The second is that in any case, we have verified that increased minimum wages are *compatible* with lower unemployment. If I am a minimum wage worker and get a fatter paycheck and there are more jobs available, why should I care if, theoretically, there would have been even more jobs available if my pay check had been thinner?

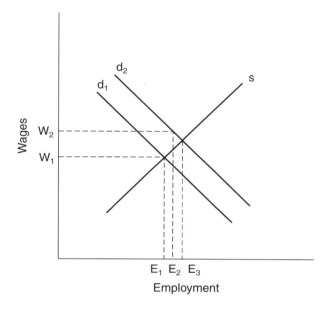

E_1 = Employment at time one (before minimum wage increase)
E_2 = Employment at time two (after minimum wage increase)
E_3 = What employment would have been at time two had there
been no minimum wage
$E_3 - E_2$ = Employment loss caused by minimum wage increase

Figure 10. Growth in Employment without a Minimum Wage
in the Conventional Model

The next group of studies seeking to tie minimum wage increases
to employment losses relied on what is called "time series" methods.
Employment (*not* unemployment) rates among a certain group are
measured immediately before and immediately after a minimum wage
increase. A series of control variables is built in for economic changes
that might also affect employment. A comparison is then drawn between the rate of employment after a minimum wage increase and what
it would have been without the increase. The group chosen for analysis was always teenagers, because a much higher percentage of them
work at the minimum wage than adults do, which makes the statisti-

cal findings more robust. Many of these studies were conducted in the 1970s. They were unanimous in their conclusion that minimum wage increases decreased teen employment, although they disagreed about the magnitude of the impairment. The degree of negative employment effects resulting from a 10 percent upward adjustment in the minimum wage ranged from 0.50 percent to 2.96 percent. Reviewing these studies in 1982, Charles Brown, Curtis Gilroy, and Andrew Kohen concluded that they showed there would be "a reduction of between one and three percent in teenage employment as a result of a 10 percent increase in the Federal minimum wage. We regard the lower part of this range as most plausible because this is what most studies, which include the experience of the 1970s and deal carefully with minimum wage coverage, tend to find."[21] In addition, other time-series studies concluded that minimum wage increases led to cuts in fringe benefits and on-the-job training.[22]

Moreover, it was often argued that if jobs are squeezed, the people most likely to feel the brunt are the least qualified. If a business has a hundred teen workers and now must lay off two, the two most likely to be discharged are the two who bring the lowest level of skills to market. Because educational levels are generally lower among minority youth, they would suffer most.

It is important to keep these studies in perspective. Even if a 1 or 2 percent reduction in teen employment occurred and even if a similar decline occurred among adults as well, not that many jobs would be affected. Gary Burtless pointed out that, with the teen figures, we are talking about five one hundredths of 1 percent of employed people, maybe less.[23] Moreover, with the rapid turnover in the low-wage job market, the chances that a diligent job seeker would be unemployed long are small. Further, the minimum wage increase would result in a higher wage for all those who initially remained employed and for those who reentered the labor force after a brief period of idleness.

For a number of years, these studies stood as the unchallenged orthodoxy in most of the economics profession. Lately, however, they have come under increased fire. First, even if the studies contain accurate conclusions regarding teenagers, there is a question whether what is true for teens is also true for adult minimum wage workers.

The teenage labor market is substantially different from the adult low-wage market. Second, doubts have been raised about the validity of the control variables. Did they, during the onset of a recession, for example, control adequately for its effects? Third, as researchers extended the period of time subject to analysis, they found diminished effects. In Allison Wellington's highly significant study that extended the time-series approach through the 1980s, she concluded that (1) a 10 percent increase in the minimum wage reduced teen employment by less than 1 percent, and because there is "withdrawal" from the market, there is no real effect on unemployment; (2) minimum wage increases of this magnitude had no effect on the employment of those 20–24 years old; and (3) there was no evidence that minority teens were affected more than white teens were.[24]

In the 1980s, scholars began using two additional approaches to limn the possible employment effects of minimum wage legislation: cross-sectional analysis and panel studies. As the federal minimum wage shrunk in effective value during the 1980s, states began raising their minimum wages. Cross-sectional studies tried to look at pooled data on states or, in one case, regions of the country.[25] Panel studies involve interviewing the same people over a period of time. Fortunately for social scientists, the National Longitudinal Studies have provided a treasure trove of data on a wide variety of subjects. Analysts have been able to delve into the employment patterns of various cohorts at the time minimum wage increases were enacted.[26] At the end of the day, however, the results of these studies are at best tentative and inconclusive.

Some studies have examined what happened in one state when the minimum wage increased, either through federal or state action. For example, Taiel Kim and Lowell Taylor analyzed the California state minimum wage hike of 1988.[27] They compared employment data for the retail sector from various counties and various types of retail businesses and concluded the act did have substantial negative employment effects. David Card and Alan Krueger later pointed out some problems with the data source Kim and Taylor used, though.[28] When Card and Krueger extended the analysis with modifications in the data, the results showed the employment effects to be statistically insignificant. Lawrence Katz and Alan Krueger tried a different tack in Texas when the federal minimum wage rose in 1991.[29] Arguing that fast-food establishments are the major employers of minimum wage labor, they surveyed a sample of fast-food restaurants before and after the increase to ascertain the number of employees they had. The results were that employment actually increased at these businesses after the jump in the minimum wage; moreover, the firms that had to raise their wages the most to meet the new minimum had the fastest rates of employment growth.

Without question, the most important book on labor economics, perhaps in the entire discipline, in over a decade is David Card and Alan Krueger's *Myth and Measurement: The New Economics of the Minimum Wage,* published in 1995. It is significant for both the method used and its substantive results. Politically, it is important because proponents of the 1996 increase constantly cited it in their briefs as evidence the minimum wage had positive employment effects, while opponents went to great lengths to discredit it. The Joint Economic Committee even called a special hearing for the book's critics to raise questions about the data set.[30]

Card and Krueger's method is the "natural experiment." In the physical sciences, controlled experimentation is the standard research procedure. To find out how a particular fertilizer affects the growth of corn, scientists plant two identical fields of corn and do the same thing to each, except that they apply the fertilizer to one (the "treatment group") and not to the other (the "control group"). Except in rare instances, such an approach is not available to social scientists.[31] The closest they can come is when two roughly similar entities adopt different policies. In 1993, New Jersey raised its state minimum wage to the highest level in the nation ($5.05), while neighboring Pennsylvania was subject only to the federal minimum (then $4.25), setting as good a stage as is likely to be found for a natural experiment.

Card and Krueger conducted two telephone surveys of fast-food establishments in the border areas of the two states, one before New Jersey's new minimum went into effect and one afterward. They asked a series of questions on the number of full-time and part-time workers, the level of fringe benefits, prices of food, and so forth. They found that employment in New Jersey actually increased after the minimum wage went up. Not only were the results predicted by the traditional model not confirmed, they were backward.

The book has been subjected to withering and fulminating critiques by various economists.[32] There are some legitimate issues regarding a few technical aspects of the surveys, and it is easy to have reservations about how sweeping a generalization can be drawn from their findings. (Some critics, for example, have contended that the conventional model predicts only that aggregate employment will fall, not what will happen in one industrial sector.) To their credit, Card and Krueger have been quite modest in their claims. Moreover, their conclusions have borne up quite well. After all the critics had their say, the most appropriate comment may have come from Richard Freeman. Their book, he said, "has shifted the burden of proof about the employment effects of the minimum wage."[33]

The most recent systematic study, by Madeline Zavodny, went back to the *County Business Patterns* data used earlier by Kim and Taylor.[34] She, too, found no significant employment effect either at the national level after the 1991 increase or in Washington State after it raised its minimum wage in 1988.

In sum, although nine decades have elapsed since Tawney thought we would soon be able to appeal to "the light of experience," we seem only marginally closer to a consensus. Taken together, the above studies and critiques do seem to leave us with four conclusions, however general and guarded:

—The evidence for a negative effect on employment is shaky, at best.
—If there are employment effects, at least at the level to which the minimum wage has been raised to date, they are small.
—A minimum wage increase has just as often been followed by a fall in unemployment rather than a rise.
—It is possible that a minimum wage increase may lead to an increase in employment.

Although this is hardly the place for a discussion of theoretical economics, it might be helpful to note briefly the condition under which

economists think a minimum wage increase could lead to an increase
in employment, Card and Krueger's finding. It relies on what is called
the "monopsony" model.[35]

Suppose, for one reason or another, the usual one given in textbooks
is a single employer in a company town, that a firm faces a limited
supply of workers. Optimally, to maximize its profits, such a business
would hire workers until the cost of adding an additional worker ex-
ceeded the revenue the worker would generate. With a restricted supply, however, raising wages does not bring more applicants. This condition is shown in figure 11. Employment, but not wages, therefore
ends up being set at the point at which marginal labor costs and marginal revenue product intersect. At that level, the firm pays a wage of
$3.00 per hour. Then Congress raises the minimum wage to $5.00 per
hour. Forced to pay the new base wage, there is movement along the

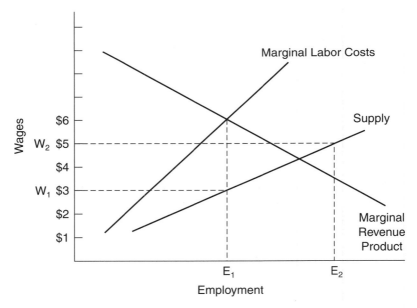

Figure 11. Monopsony and a Minimum Wage

supply curve as well. Wages go up from $3.00 to $5.00 per hour and more workers (E2) are hired.

With modifications to make it dynamic rather than static, this is the basic model that economists who believe Card and Krueger are correct are using. They are quick to point out that the minimum wage cannot rise above the point where marginal labor costs and marginal revenue are equal, $6.00 on the graph, without disemployment effects. This puts a ceiling on the theoretical level to which the minimum wage can rise; and to the extent this thinking is accepted by policymakers, it induces caution. From Secretary Reich's comments, it is clear he followed this logic, believing that there was a level to which the minimum wage could not go without causing job losses. It could be, though, that Tawney's aphorism should be followed and that thinking about labor markets should move to an even wider plane, searching for a new model instead of modifying one already in existence. If economists limit themselves to retreading monopsony, even advocates of higher minimum wages are trapped in an intellectual prison. Ideas from economics do have political consequences, and here they are decidedly limiting.

Inflation

Inflation arising from an increase in the minimum wage can be either the "cost push" or "demand pull" variety. In the former, increased costs to business are passed on to consumers in the form of price hikes. In the latter, a rise in aggregate demand with no corresponding increase in supply simply increases the prices of the available stock of goods.

It is easy to see how a minimum wage increase could lead to higher prices in the first instance. Businesses that employ minimum wage workers will try to increase their prices to recoup their increased costs. Of course, not all businesses will succeed at this game, but many will, and the cost increases will reverberate through the economy.

Demand pull inflation is a little harder to visualize. If, as many economists contend, the minimum wage redistributes income instead of increasing the size of the pie, there is no more aggregate income than there was. The reason that a minimum wage hike could lead to increased demand, however, is because of who gets the income. When people receive money (from any source), there are only two things they can do with it: spend it or save it. Generally speaking, people in higher-income brackets save a larger percentage of their incomes than do people in lower-income brackets, for obvious reasons. Imagine, now, one family of four with an income of $20,000 per year and another with $100,000 per year. If you gave each family a check for $1,000, which one would more likely spend it? Economists call this the marginal propensity to save and the marginal propensity to consume. In short, it is what you do with each additional dollar of income you receive. If the minimum wage is redistributive (a proposition for which the evidence is somewhat uncertain), it will transfer income from higher to lower brackets. All else being equal, it will therefore increase total spending and decrease total saving. The rise in consumer spending will drive prices higher, since, in theory, production is already at the "appropriate" level because of the workings of the competitive market.

It is curious that economists have not devoted more energy to analyzing the actual price effects of minimum wage increases. To return to Tawney for a moment, he found almost no price increases in the chain-making or clothing industries after the imposition of the minimum wage. There were some studies on the inflationary impact of the U.S. minimum wage done as part of the investigations ordered by Congress in the 1950s,[36] but for the most part, they were inconclusive or unconvincing.

By far the most comprehensive research on this question to date was the work done for the Minimum Wage Study Commission.[37] The people responsible for this section of the study pointed out that inflation could flow from six interrelated steps:

1. The minimum wage goes up.
2. The "ripple effect" takes place. That is, workers who were right above the old minimum now demand to be moved up above the new minimum. This leads to similar demands by those slightly above them in the wage hierarchy, and so on.
3. Every business that can raises its prices.

4. Businesses change their production methods. With the new wage schedules, it may now be profitable to buy new equipment or recruit more highly skilled labor. It is likely that these moves increase overall productivity (that is, more production per hour worked).

5. The new employment levels (if there is any unemployment resulting from the minimum wage hike) and earnings profiles change both national income and aggregate demand.

6. This may trigger new wage demands from those not directly affected by the minimum wage increase (for example, union contracts that have a built-in cost of living adjustment), which will in turn affect other wages and prices.

Using this model, the commission's staff conducted an elaborate series of studies, employing several different methodologies. In the end, the commission concluded that a 10.0 percent jump in the minimum wage leads to a "somewhat less than 0.3 percent" rise in consumer prices.[38] Clearly, minimum wage workers are much better off with the 10.0 percent pay raise.[39]

William Alpert examined prices as part of his in-depth study of the minimum wage and the restaurant industry. He reported a survey taken by the National Restaurant Association after the December 1979 minimum wage increase took effect that showed 61 percent of them had raised prices.[40] However, when he did his aggregate analyses, he found little general price movement.[41] Card and Krueger also included questions about prices in their survey. They found that the restaurants in New Jersey did increase their prices more than those in Pennsylvania, but those most affected in New Jersey (the ones with wages furthest below the new minimum) did not increase prices any more than other outlets did. It is therefore difficult to say precisely what effect the new minimum wage had on restaurant prices.[42]

Finally, Zavodny examined the prices of restaurant food and apparel (since these are two industries that employ a large portion of the minimum wage work force) using data from both the Bureau of Labor Statistics and the Chamber of Commerce from 1987 to 1992. She found slight upward movement in some but not all restaurant prices (about 1.0 to 1.5 percent) but none in the retail clothing sector.[43]

Why do price increases seem negligible or even nonexistent? One part of the answer lies in the fact that labor is only one cost factor. Say that I own a restaurant and that labor is 30 percent of my total costs (about the average for restaurants, which have one of the highest because their product is so labor intensive). Let us assume I have a 40 percent gross profit margin, not unusual for a profitable restaurant.[44] That means that for a $10.00 meal, my costs are $6.00. Of that, $1.80 represents labor. Now, suppose the minimum wage goes up 10 percent. Let us simplify and assume that everyone working in my restaurant gets a 10 percent pay raise. My labor costs will go up 18 cents, to $1.98. If all other costs remain as they were, my new cost for the meal will be $6.18 ($4.20 + $1.98). If I wish to retain the same gross profit percentage, I will have to increase my price to $10.30, a 3 percent hike. This would be the outside figure, since we raised everyone 10 percent in our example and are dealing with a high labor cost industry. For retail stores and other businesses, the impact would be less.

The other explanation is some version of the "shock theory." In neoclassical economic models, business firms operate at maximum efficiency at all times. In the real world, however, that is seldom the case. A minimum wage increase, as noted in the fourth item in the Minimum Wage Study Commission's list, will shock a business into taking action. Minimum wage workers will be better supervised or given more training. New machinery may be substituted for some labor intensive procedures. Worker morale may improve because of the higher wages. In all these cases, productivity will rise, and productivity allows a business to take in the same revenue without raising prices because it is producing more units for the same costs.

Business Failures

Predictions of business failures following in the wake of a minimum wage increase are less common than prophecies of massive job loss, but they are often made. Herman Cain, chief executive officer of Godfather's Pizza, told the Joint Economic Committee in 1995, "When you raise the cost of doing business for many thousands of businesses that are just making it—and there are thousands of small businesses that are just barely making it—you risk shutting their doors permanently."[45]

The economic logic is simple and straightforward. In neoclassical theory, all firms are already operating at maximum internal efficiency, and their prices are set by the competitive markets in which they sell their products or services. If the cost of a production factor—in this case, labor—rises, the increase must be met somehow. One option is attempted price hikes. However, this will lead some consumers to buy other products, unit sales will fall, and some firms will have to close. Layoffs or reductions in hours worked by employees is another option. But this means fewer customers can be served. Business will fall off, and the less efficient companies will close. Labor-saving devices can be introduced to cut labor costs, but this requires capital, which some firms do not have and cannot obtain. Thus, the less well capitalized will go under.

Somewhat surprisingly, there are only four analyses of how profits and business failures might be affected by minimum wage increases. One is William Alpert's examination of the effects of the minimum wage on the restaurant industry. While he focused on employment patterns, he also built a model predicting the number of restaurant failures. He then used the actual rate of failures as reported by Dun and Bradstreet, the financial reporting firm, to test his predictions. He concluded, "While the differences between actual and predicted failures are not statistically significant, the predicted failure rate is usually below the actual failure rate. All in all, there is minimal evidence that the minimum wage has affected restaurant sales or profits. . . . We find no evidence that the minimum wage has lowered restaurant sales or profits."[46]

Card and Krueger examined the possible effects of minimum wage increases on the stock prices of publicly traded companies (110 in all) that employ significant numbers of minimum wage workers.[47] If investors believed that profits were going to fall, they presumably would sell the stock, driving the price down. Because the stock market is driven more heavily by news of what might happen than by actual events, it would be illogical to measure stock prices before and after the increase took effect. Instead, they sought out instances when politicians signaled they were considering raising the minimum wage. They found only very modest effects: "In the sample of events that we have examined, news about a minimum-wage hike rarely seems to coincide with movements of more than 1 or 2 percent in shareholder wealth."[48]

Two colleagues and I conducted the third study. We relied on the total business failure rate as reported by Dun and Bradstreet from 1949 to 1984.[49] We first compared the average (mean) failure rate for years in which there was no minimum wage increase against the years in which the increases occurred and the years immediately following. We found no significant difference between the normal business failure rate and the failure rate in the years in which increases went into effect and the lag years. Second, we ran a multiple regression to see if the size of the minimum wage hike affected the business failure rate in any way. This exercise showed that higher minimum wage increases had no more impact on business failures than lower ones. In short, there is no significant historical relationship between minimum wage increases and the business failure rate, no matter what the level of the increase.

Zavodny also analyzed this issue. She examined the total number of eating and drinking establishments rather than the failure rate. She found that the number of eating and drinking places actually grew after the 1991 minimum wage increase. "The results," she said, "indicate that a 10 percent increase in the minimum wage is correlated with about a 1 to 1.7 percent increase in the number of eating/drinking places."[50]

All four of these studies are preliminary and cannot be used to form unchallengeable conclusions. It is, however, noteworthy that all four point in the same direction: minimum wages either have little role or have a positive role in sustaining business activity. Theoretically, two sets of explanations can be adduced for what, by the conventional model, is an anomalous result. The first is that businesses increase productivity in response to minimum wage increases, as laid out in the previous section. The other is that the increased purchasing power generated by jumps in the minimum wage increases business revenues enough overall to offset or perhaps even exceed the increased costs.[51]

Reducing Poverty

Any discussion of the relationship between higher minimum wages and a reduction in poverty must necessarily be tentative because we are in the midst of a major transformation of the nation's welfare system. We must therefore distinguish between what was true before and what may happen in the future. In the past, analysts of this problem typically began by stating that two-thirds of poor adults did not work. Any impact of an elevated minimum wage on poverty rates (unless it was set high enough to stimulate substantially higher labor market participation) was thus bound to be limited. In the future, though, if all goes as planned, the percentage of poor adults who work will rise significantly. We can offer only the most guarded of speculations on what the outcome of this project will be, for it is far too early even to know all the ramifications of the route we have taken.

Ideally, to assay the effects of the minimum wage on poverty, a researcher would have to (1) separate minimum wage workers who live in families that are in poverty from those who do not; (2) ascertain how much the minimum wage workers in poverty contribute to family income; (3) compute the additional earnings these minimum wage workers bring home after an increase; and (4) find out how many families this moves above the poverty line. The first can be done because the Current Population Survey now matches individuals with family earnings. The second and third calculations are fraught with difficulty, however. Should the ripple effect be included? Can we assume that hours worked will be the same? And so on. Finally, the last item requires estimations of family size, among other things. All told, it is a knotty and tricky undertaking.

In 1980, Donald Parsons attempted the first major systematic study of this issue. He used the National Longitudinal Survey of Females to trace what happened to adult females over the decade following the 1967 minimum wage boost. He concluded that the minimum wage had served to raise the average wages of low-skilled adult females, but only slightly. When he looked at the families in which those women lived, however, he found little evidence of falling poverty rates attributable to the minimum wage. "Indeed, the evidence suggests that the minimum wage laws affect poverty, even among working adults, hardly at all."[52]

The most often cited study to date was done by Ronald Mincy in 1990.[53] He began by noting that there are three barriers to using the minimum wage as a poverty-fighting tool: (1) the extent of coverage and compliance with the law, (2) the "characteristics of low-wage workers," and (3) the attributes of poor families containing low-wage workers. He constructed an elaborate model and applied it to Current Population Survey data for 1987, running the model with several alternative scenarios. The two most important factors he varied were the extent of the law's coverage and the "elasticity" of the disemployment effect. Recall that in 1987 retail and service firms grossing less than $362,500 were exempt from the Fair Labor Standards Act. Not knowing how many minimum wage workers were employed by such companies, Mincy ran different percentages, including an assumption of full coverage (removal of the exemption). Since we now have, as a result of a Department of Labor ruling and the failure of the Goodling and Bond amendments in 1996, virtually full coverage, it is these estimates that are most germane. As of 1990, the accepted relationship between minimum wage increases and job losses was a 1–3 percent reduction in teenage employment for every 10 percent hike in the minimum wage, which Brown, Gilroy, and Kohen summarized. Fortunately, though, in the interest of thoroughness, Mincy ran the model with no employment effects. His conclusion was that if the minimum wage had been $4.25 in 1987 (it was $3.35), with full coverage and compliance and no job loss, there would have been an 11.1 percent reduction in the poverty gap (the difference between the poverty line for each family in poverty summed and their current incomes summed) for families with at least one low-wage worker and that the number of these families in poverty would have fallen by 8.7 percent. Since a jump to $4.25 represented a 27 percent increase, these figures seem depressingly low. It bears stressing again that these numbers are for families with someone working at a low-wage job, not the total of all poor families.

Card and Krueger included a brief exercise on the minimum wage's role in reducing poverty in their book. They first examined the poverty rates by state before and after the minimum wage increase of 1990. Even after they adjusted for the effects of other economic factors that might have influenced poverty rates, they found that the percentage of people in poverty did decline most sharply in the states most affected by the minimum wage increase. They then calculated the *maximum* percentage of the working poor who could have been elevated out of poverty by a $4.25 minimum wage in 1990. They reported that their analysis showed it hovered around 12 percent. In sum, while there was certainly no evidence that a higher minimum wage increased poverty (as one might gather from those who argue that large job losses will ensue), they maintained that there is only "a modest poverty-reducing effect of the minimum wage."[54]

Deborah Figart and June Lapidus examined the value of raising the minimum wage versus adopting comparable worth as a tool for reducing poverty among women.[55] One interesting technical aspect of their work was an attempt to include the ripple effect. They estimated that raising the minimum wage to $4.75 (from $4.25) would reduce the percentage of adult women in poverty by about 3 or 4 percentage points.

In sum, all pre–welfare reform studies showed only small reductions in poverty resulting from minimum wage boosts. What about the future, though?

Much of how one feels about the likelihood that longtime welfare recipients will be gainfully employed when the time limits expire depends on why one thinks they were not working in the first place.

It is clear that if work is going to be substituted for welfare *and* move people out of poverty, it must pay adequately. If there had never been public assistance or a minimum wage, perhaps all the poor would now be working; but they might be—no, almost certainly would be—still poor. In an objective economic sense, if the minimum wage were to be set so that one wage earner could make enough with one full-time year-round job to lift a family of three above the poverty threshold, and if such a minimum wage job were available to anyone who wanted it, all families of three would be removed from the stigma of poverty.

What if a minimum wage job does not meet that level (as it currently does not)? What about families with more than three people? What about child care and medical costs? What if there is not an adequate number of living wage jobs? Finally, what if there is an ample supply of such jobs, but former welfare recipients do not take or stay in them?

It could be that welfare reform may influence minimum wage politics profoundly. If work is to be commanded, how far below the poverty line should a family with one, one and a half, or two people making the minimum wage be allowed to sink? As it is, there are more pressing concerns, the fate of the hard-core unemployed when the clock ticks down and what will happen if the economy turns down. In the long run, though, the tie between the minimum wage and lifting people out of poverty, one of the original aims of both the Progressive reformers and the New Deal backers of the minimum wage, may be reestablished.

Conclusion

From the perspective of the political system as a whole, we are left with a policy that has either unknown or trivial effects on employment, inflation, business failures, and poverty. There is consequently a political stillness regarding the minimum wage almost immediately after a presidential signing ceremony. If a rise in unemployment could be traced to the minimum wage, there would be political fallout, because the public always responds to rising unemployment.[56] Politicians, for their part, also always take note. As it is, though, all discussion of possible job losses or gains resulting from an increase in the minimum wage soon dissipates. Should inflation spiral upward, and if any portion of the increase was reliably laid at the feet of the minimum wage, the politically relevant strata would surely let that be known. But how, if at all, the minimum wage contributes to inflation also soon recedes into the background. Most certainly, if business failures rose and anyone thought there was even the remotest possibility that the minimum wage was responsible, the pressure would come swiftly and would be overwhelming. As for the social welfare coalition, it, too, soon pushes the minimum wage aside. Its energy has historically focused on other issues: Aid to Families with Dependent Children, food stamps, public housing, Pell Grants, and the like.[57] Few members of Congress who vote for a minimum wage increase or their supporters in think tanks and the media seem to give it much thought afterward. To policymakers and the politically vocal segments of society, the minimum wage is about ideology and symbolism, with no effects worth expending political energy on.

One afternoon during my tenure as a subminimum wage worker, a coworker asked me to cover for her for a minute while she called to check on her young son who had stayed home from school that day. "Is he sick?" I asked. "No," she replied, "there was a field trip to a museum and I didn't have the money for the admission." How many children got to go on a field trip or perhaps to a movie in 1996 and 1997 that they would have missed had it not been for the minimum wage hike? How many people had a warmer coat this winter than last? How many people finally got to buy that new piece of furniture from Wal-Mart or save for the down payment on a mobile home? Of course, some of the increase went for wasteful or even harmful items, such as cigarettes and tattoos, but at the same time it gave many people just a little more control over their world.

In short, for the 10 million Americans who got a raise in 1996 and 1997, the minimum wage was neither ideological nor symbolic and certainly not without an impact. Their disconnectedness from the political system, however, ensures that the field trip, the coat, the furniture, and the mobile home will be enjoyed without even a ripple being made on the political waters.

CONCLUSION

The minimum wage was initiated in the United States by middle-class Progressive reformers. Few labor leaders were interested in the idea, and those few had serious reservations. After a round of early successes in the states, the minimum wagers, as Vivien Hart called them,[1] were overwhelmed by the onset of World War I and the economic conservatism that followed in its wake. The minimum wage found public favor once again when the Great Depression struck. State minimum wage laws spread in the early 1930s, and the idea was included in the Roosevelt administration's first major attack on unemployment, the National Industrial Recovery Act. In 1938, Congress was persuaded to adopt a standard national minimum wage of twenty-five cents an hour in the aptly titled Fair Labor Standards Act. Although its reach was far from universal, the outlines of the policy were set. Proponents clearly hoped the future would find a higher wage level and increased coverage.

Since then, American political life has been periodically punctuated by conflict over those two issues. With the exception of 1949, there has been a tendency to raise the wage and cover more workers. Today, the wage level stands at roughly twice its 1938 value in constant dollars, and only a few minute corners of the economy are not covered.

It is an undeniably popular policy. Huge majorities of the public favor the program, and most believe it should be strengthened by granting a considerably higher wage. Even among groups that show low support, a sizable majority still backs the program. This support remains even when people know they must pay the costs. Few other public policies enjoy this level of public approval.

The low public saliency of the issue, however, disconnects this broad public support from the actual politics of the program. When a minimum wage increase is debated in Congress, it takes on an ideological and symbolic character. Opponents assail the ideological impurity it represents and take umbrage at the way it intrudes into business decision making. Business trade groups affected by the measure—the retail and restaurant industries, in particular—combine with ideological allies to fight bitterly against any increase. Proponents do not burn with the same ideological fervor but will eagerly join a fight for a hike. The symbolic aspects of the policy are as important to them as any real effect it might have. Supported by civil rights and women's groups, along with unions, they often manage to garner enough votes from moderate members of Congress to secure a middling increase.

Because the proponents' major attention is focused elsewhere, however, they do not push the program regularly. Instead, it lies almost dormant most of the time, until political conditions open a window onto the active agenda. It is never entirely dormant, because someone is almost always suggesting an increase. Such demands are ordinarily ignored, though. Only when "enablers," politicians with high public visibility, take up the issue and trigger public and political consciousness does a serious possibility exist for an increase. Even after the enablers move the issue to the active agenda, there is still the bruising legislative battle to fight. Because of the endless complications of American politics, the outcome is never certain. Despite extremely high public approval, the internal political coalitions in Congress and the relationship between Congress and the president largely determine the outcome. The public's feelings are background noise, providing political ammunition for the supporters of an increase, but they do not seem to have much direct effect on the legislative process.

Almost immediately after the minimum wage partisans win an increase, the issue all but disappears. Politicians on both sides more or less forget about it, and the victors often do not even claim credit. Interest groups return to their core concerns, and public interest recedes. Until instigators convince a new group of enablers to pick the matter up, it sleeps.

Two groups of people do maintain a strong interest in the minimum wage, though. Economists are reflexively drawn to the program since it is such an anomaly. The grip of neoclassical and welfare economics is so strong that analyzing the employment effects of the policy is irresistible. Although less often discussed, how inflation and business failures are affected by minimum wage increases is equally interesting theoretically. Few economists, it seems, fail to have an interest in or an opinion about the matter.

The other group that has an interest are low-wage workers and their employers. Talk to people working in any retail business or restaurant, and you will find that they are keenly aware of the minimum wage. They know precisely when it is going up and by how much. Their families, too, know, understand, and care deeply. Business people in these industries also follow the vagaries of the minimum wage.

The program is thus not without effects or without a group of people who follow it. Neither economists nor minimum wage workers, however, have any direct influence on political decision makers when it comes to initiating policies. Further, the negligible effects the program seems to have on business means that few employers spend much time worrying about the level of the minimum wage once an increase goes into effect.

Symbolic Policies and Symbolic Politics

I argued in the introduction that symbolic policy deserves the status of a separate category in the Lowi typology, standing with constituent and suasive policies in a noncoercive grouping. If such a category is justified, what types of politics would be found here? Is there a distinction between those cases where the analyst and the participants agree that the policy is chiefly symbolic and those instances in which the analyst sees another category and the participants see symbolism?

Simon Harrison, an anthropologist, has done the most extensive work on political conflicts over symbols. He breaks the political contests over symbols down into four types. The first of these is what he calls *valuation*, where the question is the ranking of the symbols of competing groups. Among the examples he provides is the protracted struggle in mid-eighteenth-century France over the merits of French versus Italian music, a dispute that finally had to be settled by the king. The two types of music, it seems, symbolized order and hierarchy versus an emerging egalitarianism. A second type of symbolic conflict he labels *proprietary*. The quarrel here centers on ownership of a symbol. A cogent example is a recent attempt by Northern Ireland's Protestants to adopt an eighth-century Irish chieftain named Cuchulain, a move strongly resisted by Irish Catholics, who view him as an indigenous folk hero.

Innovation contests constitute the third cluster, which occur when polities or groups within them try to outdo each other with symbolic trappings, as when nineteenth-century European coronation ceremonies grew in pomp and elaborateness. The last type is the *expansionary* contest, in which one group seeks to replace another's symbols with one or more of its own. The renaming of St. Petersburg as Leningrad and then back again is a case in point.

It is easy to think of modern-day counterparts to all these types in contemporary Western democracies. The politics spawned by such battles ordinarily parallel what T. Alexander Smith found when he studied "emotive symbolic" policies. These struggles, he said, "tend to be characterized by high levels of intensity and broad scopes of conflict, for they activate large numbers of citizens who feel deeply about the particular issues in question."[2]

However, this description does not mesh with what was presented in the preceding pages. We did not encounter large numbers of people activated by deep feelings. Instead, we found people with unambiguous but shallow feelings hardly activated at all. We discovered a relatively high level of intensity, but its duration was extremely brief. Further, a clash over raising the minimum wage certainly touched off no broader conflict. To explain why minimum wage politics is so different from these other types of symbolic politics, it is necessary to refer to the analyst versus participant distinction developed in the introduction. That is, there are cases when both an outside observer and the participants in the political process agree that the policy is symbolic, while there are also cases in which an objective evaluation of the policy would put it in the regulatory or redistributive category, but the participants view it as symbolic.

The first situation might be called the politics of *primary* symbolism. What is at issue is understood by all concerned, as in all of Harrison's types. Given people's strong attachment to symbols, if political conflict is unleashed, it is likely to follow the patterns Smith depicted. One need only think of the school prayer controversy in the United States, for example. When the objective situation and the participant's view of the matter diverge, however, setting up what might profitably be called the politics of *secondary* symbolism, several differences emerge.

The first is that the political contestants might see the policy differently. While there are always some differences in how participants in politics define an issue, there is a broad consensus on what is at stake in primary symbolic politics. When regulatory or redistributive policies (as defined by an observer) are on the table, though, some of the participants might also see it as wholly or partially regulatory or redistributive even while others see it as symbolic. Alternatively or even at the same time, participants might all see the issue as symbolic but have different symbols in mind. Either way, the debate is likely to be more garbled and filled with more static than when the symbols are sharply focused and well understood. The politics are therefore likely to be rather fluid.

As for the public, the lack of a clearly defined symbol leads to more quiescence than when primary symbolic politics erupts. The more complex an issue, the harder it is for the public to frame it in the simplistic, unambiguous manner needed for moral stances to harden. Messages from the political elite can confuse or clarify issues for the public, and the less the political elite agrees about what is driving an issue, the less the public will be moved to intensity. Moreover, any policy involving money is less likely to provoke moral outrage than a purely symbolic policy would.

What results is a politics with two chief characteristics. The first is temporary intensity. Even if only some of the participants see an issue in symbolic and moral terms, they can raise the level of political conflict. This happens in minimum wage politics, as diehard free marketeers insist the matter has a moral dimension. Try as the pro–minimum wage forces may to defuse this position by referring to inflation adjustments and so forth, it cannot be silenced. The second is low public involvement. For one thing, those most helped by the policy are largely without political voice. Furthermore, while the public's stance is manifestly clear, the muddying effect of elite arguments and the sheer fact that the minimum wage does not pose an immediate moral question to many people lower the salience of the public's views. The message from the public to the politicians is therefore clear but not loud. Consequently, those making the actual decisions—chiefly members of Congress but also the president and his advisers—need take only marginal notice of the public's wishes. Those wishes are not totally insignificant, but they do not impinge directly on those in power.

The result is a politics of rigidity for many but flexibility for a few. The positions of those participants who are true believers on both sides are carved in stone. They cannot be moved by public sentiment, political calculations, or the urgings of party leaders. Those with fewer ideological proclivities—who do not see the issue as so strongly symbolic—move with one side or the other as political calculation or conscience dictates.

Because the minimum wage is either regulatory or redistributive (depending on your view of the economics) in actual substance, though, its effects are real even if its politics are symbolic. This clearly differentiates all secondary symbolic politics from the primary variety. Music, a folk hero, a coronation, and a city's name all have consequences to be sure, especially if one takes a rather long-term perspective. However, the consequences flow chiefly from how people feel. Secondary symbolic politics, in contrast, produces policies that have immediate tangible results. Secondary symbolic politics is important not only because tangible effects flow from whatever decisions are taken but also because participants approach a policy as a window onto their understandings of a just political order.

Resurrecting the Political Economy of Citizenship

What is most revealing and striking, and in many ways most determinative, about the minimum wage is the conceptual framework its friends bring to it. On all major congressional votes since 1938, the minimum wage coalition invariably includes those from the left of the Democratic party to moderate Republicans, losing a few Democrats here and there. This is, of course, the normal pattern on both economic regulatory and social welfare issues, and the minimum wage encompasses both. Support for these policies is firm on the Democratic left and soft in the party's center and the Republican left. If enough of the moderates from both parties can be coaxed along, economic regulatory and social welfare policies can carry the day. It is true-blue economic liberals on the left of the Democratic party, though, who must provide the political energy for these policies, and political energy is ultimately generated by ideas.

The Progressives who imported and built the minimum wage house carried a view of political economy that was partly influenced by civic republicanism. They did not detach economic analysis from the public good, broadly conceived. They did not wish to raise the incomes of the poor solely to give them more consumption choices. A person's identity, if not the individual's soul, was at stake, for they believed that poverty stunted the finer aspects of human character. They therefore did not see the minimum wage merely or even largely as a cash transfer program. It was built on a feeling that people who worked had a dignity as people that was eroded by sweatshop conditions and the lives generated by substandard wages. A minimum wage was a way to give worth and dignity to individuals. The first Massachusetts statute, recall, said that the wage should be set at a level sufficient "to supply the necessary cost of living and to maintain the worker in health."

The New Deal's intellectual architects advocated both economic regulation and mild redistribution. Their goals were more straightforwardly economic than those of their Progressive forebears, but bringing the country out of the Great Depression took such a high priority that this is not surprising. Even so, there were scattered discussions of citizenship values, and they certainly never envisaged government transfer programs as the centerpiece of social welfare policy.[3]

Modern social welfare liberals, however, judge policies largely by two criteria: how they affect the relative and absolute distribution of wealth and how economically efficient they are. The value premises underlying the second thrust are obviously a nod to neoclassical economics. The other rests on a principle of "fairness," but it is an idea of fairness that is inchoate and unsatisfying, for it rests on no absolute sense of justice. Social welfare liberals shy away from absolute values generally, since as good classical liberals, they view individual preferences as unchallengeable. Instead, procedures become the ultimate measuring rod under this approach, which means economic justice (or any other kind) cannot have an absolute status.

A political economy of citizenship, drawing on a civic republican rather than an individualistic framework, would serve minimum wage advocates better and recast the debate. When people are considered citizens rather than self-interested individuals, the character of politics and the appropriate ends of public policy both change. The search for the common good replaces interest articulation, and how the state should nurture and maintain a virtuous citizenry becomes a legitimate topic for public policy.

Adopting such a focus would elevate the minimum wage to a more prominent place in the policy folder than it now holds. Rather than an adjunct to transfer and directly redistributional policies, it would become a major issue of public debate. What, after all, it would ask, is the role of the individual citizen as a worker in the economy?

It would also put the social value of work on the agenda.[4] How does work relate to citizenship? Who should be expected to work? Can work, even work that is unpleasant, be given more dignity by changing its remuneration? Does someone who works exert a claim on the society for a wage that supports "the normal needs of the average employee regarded as a human being living in a civilized community" (the Australian standard)?

Moreover, it would rekindle the old Jeffersonian arguments about the connection between property, independence, and citizenship. Jefferson and his followers thought that small farmers were the best citizens not only because they were not dependent on others for their livelihoods but also because independence and property ownership nurtured the character traits necessary for a healthy citizenship.[5] Property ownership, according to many civic republicans of the period, builds a sturdiness of character and ensures a deep tie to the community. If we substitute a measure of economic security for property, are not the same arguments germane today? If so, to what degree should public policy encourage or provide a measure of earned economic security for all citizens? Is not the minimum wage perhaps the best way to do that without creating a sense of dependency? If dependency develops, then of course the very argument for economic security as an aid to citizenship is destroyed.

Finally, there is the issue of the political implications of economic inequality. Modern liberals repeatedly decry economic inequality. But, again, unless one believes economic inequality results from an unfair process, how can a system built on relative values contend it is bad? Beginning with the political, however, leads to the observation that extreme economic inequality has two decidedly negative consequences for citizenship. First, neither luxury nor poverty is hospitable to republican citizenship. The sober virtues needed to maintain a system of ordered liberty and widespread participation guided by a search for the public interest find barren soil in both states. Second, vast economic inequalities undermine the public institutional space necessary to civic equality.[6] Civic republicanism requires more than one person one vote. Institutions such as schools, parks, transportation facilities, and the military are not constructed primarily to deliver services. Their value is not expressed in market terms. A civic republic establishes a significant number of places where citizens meet as equals, unaffected by money or status. To the extent economic inequality erodes these common social spaces, citizenship is damaged. In what ways could a minimum wage reduce economic inequality and thereby contribute to a healthier civic life? Suppose it could be demonstrated that a higher minimum wage meant lower economic growth. Would the citizenry sacrifice some growth to maintain the viability of republican institutions and a measure of citizen equality?

Two trends may be pushing modern minimum wagers toward reconsidering the political economy of citizenship. First is Americans' renewed interest in civic republicanism. Across the political spectrum, it is becoming a noticeably important strain of the public debate.[7] The second is welfare reform. As people are transferred from public assistance to work, the issues of the dignity of work and its appropriate remuneration will inevitably arise. People who work will have a stronger moral and political claim to a decent living than welfare recipients ever did, and it is a claim that inescapably raises deep issues of citizenship.

Students of public welfare have begun to skate around the outer edges of this issue. One example is Nancy Fraser's effort to explain how equality, especially gender equality, fares under different models for distributing welfare benefits.[8] She posits the universal breadwinner model and the caregiver parity model, the former brimming with features that could pull together citizenship and the minimum wage. Her chief concern, however, is still how these pull the welfare state to confer monetary benefits in public programs, not how work, character, and political equality broadly conceived touch fundamental matters of political theory. Citizenship, in contrast to need and desert, she writes plainly, "allocates provision on the basis of membership in society."[9] Until the universal breadwinner model is linked to other facets of citizenship, this approach will remain a version of social welfare liberalism, a mere simulacrum of civic republicanism.

More directly pertinent is Lawrence Mead's recent work on the reinstatement of paternalism in welfare policy. Concerned for a number of years about the link between welfare benefits and citizens' obligations, he now points to a new attempt to regulate the behavior of those who receive the welfare state's monies.[10] The old paternalism was a none-too-subtle attempt to regulate directly the mores of the poor, a system that broke down in the more libertarian sixties. The new paternalism derives from a belief that the tendency not to work has deleterious effects on the poor themselves and, in turn, the larger society. It, too, is an attempt to modify behavior but largely on contractual terms. The bargain is, "You may have benefits, but you must work." The character traits, or at least the behavioral patterns, that will ensue raise the odds that recipients will become contributing members of society and lift themselves out of poverty. While Mead himself does not speak explicitly of civic republicanism, James Q. Wilson does in a concluding essay in Mead's edited book on the subject.[11] Although Wilson's discussion is rather brief, the civic republican label is decidedly on the table. Still, there is no mention of how the minimum wage ties into such an approach.

Interestingly, the public seems ahead of the political elite on this topic. The polls cited in chapter 3 show that the American public respects work and that they believe it should be adequately remunerated.

Further, they seem prepared to bear the costs of paying people a decent wage if necessary. Surely, the political debate over the minimum wage will match up with these values at some point.

Two caveats must be added at this point. First, a political economy of citizenship will not replace the purely economic issues that now dominate the debate over the minimum wage. There are legitimate theoretical and practical questions about the minimum wage's employment effects, its impact on inflation, and its possible role in business failures. The political economy of citizenship allows ample room for continued inquiry into these matters. It is simply that these discussions will have to stand alongside fundamental political issues.

Second, it is unlikely that debates over minimum wage issues conditioned by the political economy of citizenship will be any more consensual than the current dialogue is. Simply because people agree on what the issues are does not mean that they agree on solutions or tradeoffs. All of the questions posed earlier elicit sharp differences of opinion among people of goodwill. What the minimum wage should be would still trigger a heated partisan struggle, as it should in a healthy democracy.

E. J. Dionne has written, "Talk of citizenship and civic virtue sounds utopian. In fact, it is the essence of practical politics. Only by restoring our sense of common citizenship can we hope to deal with the most profound—and practical—issues before us."[12] If we begin drawing on the civic republican tradition and approach the minimum wage from the perspective of the political economy of citizenship, it would signify a return to the policy's Progressive heritage, and its politics would undoubtedly change dramatically.

NOTES

Introduction

1. Theodore J. Lowi, "American Business, Public Policy, Case Studies, and Political Theory," *World Politics* 16 (1964): 677–715.

2. Ibid., 690.

3. Ibid.

4. Theodore J. Lowi, "Four Systems of Policy, Politics, and Choice," *Public Administration Review* 32 (1972): 298–310.

5. Theodore J. Lowi, foreword to *Social Regulatory Policy: Moral Controversies in American Politics,* ed. Raymond Tatalovich and Byron Daynes (Boulder, Colo.: Westview, 1988), x–xxi.

6. Robert Spitzer, *The Presidency and Public Policy: The Four Arenas of Presidential Power* (Tuscaloosa: University of Alabama Press, 1983), chap. 2; Robert Spitzer, "Promoting Policy Theory: Reforming the Arenas of Power," *Policy Studies Journal* 15 (1987): 675–89.

7. Lowi, foreword, x.

8. Spitzer, *Presidency and Public Policy,* 27.

9. James L. Anderson, "Governmental Suasion: Refocusing the Lowi Policy Typology," *Policy Studies Journal* 25 (1997): 266–82.

10. Theodore J. Lowi, "Comments on Anderson's 'Governmental Suasion: Adding to the Lowi Policy Typology,'" *Policy Studies Journal* 25 (1997): 283–85.

11. Anderson, "Response to Theodore J. Lowi's 'Comments,'" *Policy Studies Journal* 26 (1997): 557.

12. T. Alexander Smith, *The Comparative Policy Process* (Santa Barbara, Calif.: ABC-Clio, 1975).

13. James B. Christoph, *Capital Punishment and British Politics* (Chicago: University of Chicago Press, 1962).

14. Simon Harrison, "Four Types of Symbolic Conflict," *Journal of the Royal Anthropological Institute* 2 (1995): 255–72.

15. I am aware that this omits the concept of a "nondecision" from public policy. That is, a policy decision could be to leave some area of life to the market or to private choice. For the moment, however, this definition will

suffice. For an elaboration of decisions versus nondecisions, see Peter Bachrach and Morton Baratz, "Two Faces of Power," *American Political Science Review* 56 (1962): 947–52.

16. Aynsley Kellow, "Promoting Elegance in Policy Theory: Simplifying Lowi's Arenas of Power," *Policy Studies Journal* 16 (1988): 713–24. See also Jerrold Schneider, *Ideological Coalitions in Congress* (Westport, Conn.: Greenwood, 1979).

17. Theodore J. Lowi, "An Assessment of Kellow's 'Promoting Elegance in Policy Theory,'" *Policy Studies Journal* 16 (1988): 725, 727.

18. Raymond Tatalovich and Byron Daynes, "Introduction: What Is Social Regulatory Policy?" in *Social Regulatory Policy*, ed. Tatalovich and Daynes, 1. Robert Spitzer, however, classifies it as redistributive. See Spitzer, *Presidency and Public Policy*, 163.

19. Lowi, "American Business, Public Policy, Case Studies, and Political Theory."

20. Smith, *Comparative Policy Process*, 3.

Chapter 1: The Politics of Ideas

1. This act, along with the other Australian and New Zealand laws, is discussed in Barbara Armstrong, *Insuring the Essentials: Minimum Wage Plus Social Insurance* (New York: Macmillan, 1932), part 2, section 4. See also Russell Ward, *A Nation for a Continent: The History of Australia, 1901–1975* (Richmond, Victoria: Heinemann, 1977), 45–50.

2. The league's activities are discussed briefly in Armstrong, *Insuring the Essentials*, 60–62, and more thoroughly in Vivien Hart, *Bound by Our Constitution: Women, Workers, and the Constitution* (Princeton, N.J.: Princeton University Press, 1994), 65–83.

3. *Muller v. Oregon*, 208 U.S. 412 (1908).

4. Hart, *Bound by Our Constitution*, argues that the constitutional strictures ultimately redounded to the minimum wage advocate's favor, unlike in Great Britain. Once the minimum wage was upheld by the Supreme Court, it gained a cloak of legitimacy the British statute could never obtain.

5. Two good summaries of Progressivism, especially of the historiography, are David M. Kennedy, "Progressivism: An Overview," *Historian* 37 (1975): 453–68; and Daniel Rodgers, "In Search of Progressivism," *Reviews in American History* 10 (1982): 113–32. Morton Keller's *Regulating the New Economy* (Cambridge, Mass.: Harvard University Press, 1990) is helpful on economic affairs. Eldon Eisenach's *The Lost Promise of Progressivism* (Lawrence: Uni-

versity Press of Kansas, 1994) is a lively and original piece of scholarship. James Kloppenberg's *Uncertain Victory: Social Democracy and Progressivism in European and American Thought, 1870–1920* (New York: Oxford University Press, 1986) provides a much needed comparative dimension. An excellent recent study is Daniel Rodgers, *Atlantic Crossings: Social Politics in a Progressive Age* (Cambridge, Mass.: Harvard University Press, 1998).

6. See, for example, Peter Filene, "An Obituary for the Progressive Movement," *American Quarterly* 22 (1970): 20–34.

7. A good study of the Social Gospel is Susan Curtis, *A Consuming Faith: The Social Gospel and Modern America* (Baltimore: Johns Hopkins University Press, 1991). Although it concentrates heavily on the fine arts, Robert Crunden's *Ministers of Reform: The Progressives' Achievement in American Civilization, 1889–1920* (Urbana: University of Illinois Press, 1984) also merits attention.

8. Eisenach, *Lost Promise of Progressivism*, 31–36. E. R. A. Seligman, who was Jewish, was the only non-Protestant.

9. John R. Commons and John B. Andrews, *Principles of Labor Legislation* (New York: Harper and Brothers, 1916), 24.

10. Kloppenberg, *Uncertain Victory,* 173.

11. The best general summary of the Progressive approach to political economy is Richard T. Ely, *The Past and Present of Political Economy,* Johns Hopkins University Studies in Historical and Political Science, series 2, no. 3 (Baltimore: Johns Hopkins University, 1884), 5–64.

12. A brief discussion of classical economics is Takashi Negishi, *History of Economic Theory* (Amsterdam: North-Holland, 1989), 71–190. A good source for a more detailed analysis is Joseph Schumpeter's magisterial *History of Economic Analysis* (New York: Oxford University Press, 1954). Readable accounts of the life and thought of the major economists are in Robert Heilbroner, *The Worldly Philosophers,* 6th ed. (New York: Touchstone Books, 1987).

13. Ely, *Past and Present of Political Economy,* 39.

14. Sidney Fine, *Laissez-Faire and the General Welfare State* (Ann Arbor: University of Michigan Press, 1956), 201.

15. For a thorough analysis, see Kloppenberg, *Uncertain Victory.* See also Thomas McCraw, *Prophets of Regulation* (Cambridge, Mass.: Harvard University Press, 1984).

16. The minimum wage was discussed in the following works: Commons and Andrews, *Principles of Labor Legislation,* chap. 4; Arthur Holcombe, "The Legal Minimum Wage in the United States," *American Economic Re-*

view 2 (1912): 21–37; Walter Lippmann, "The Campaign against Sweating," *New Republic*, March 27, 1915, part 2, 1–8; Henry Rogers Seager, "The Theory of the Minimum Wage," *American Labor Legislation Review* 3 (1913): 81–91; and the discussion that followed Seager's paper (originally delivered at a conference of the American Association for Labor Legislation), published in the same issue of the *Review*. The most comprehensive contemporary critique is John Bates Clark, "The Minimum Wage," *Atlantic Monthly*, September 1913, 289–97.

17. Quoted in the discussion on the minimum wage published in *American Labor Legislation Review* 3 (1913): 110.

18. Holcombe, "Legal Minimum Wage in the United States," 33.

19. Samuel Gompers and most union leaders were opposed to the minimum wage at this time. They reasoned that a legally established minimum wage would tend to become the maximum wage. They thought that collective bargaining was a much better route to better wages. Many Progressives therefore went to some lengths to refute the idea that the minimum would become the maximum. On Gompers's hostility to the minimum wage, see Bernard Mandel, *Samuel Gompers: A Biography* (Yellow Springs, Ohio: Antioch, 1963), 174–80.

20. Discussion in *American Labor Legislation Review*, 109.

21. Holcombe, "Legal Minimum Wage in the United States," 34.

22. Commons and Andrews, *Principles of Labor Legislation*, 193.

23. Ibid., 190.

24. Quoted in Eisenach, *Lost Promise of Progressivism*, 169.

25. Seager, "Theory of the Minimum Wage," 88.

26. See particularly Holcombe, "Legal Minimum Wage in the United States"; and Lippmann, "Campaign against Sweating." They also recognized that a minimum wage might have to be supplemented by controls on immigration if it were to work. This point has led some critics to argue the Progressives were nativists and racists. Perhaps they had strains of those ideas, but they were virtually all cosmopolitan people. Nonetheless, they recognized quite clearly that unlimited immigration of the type often found during this period—contract immigration whereby industrial concerns blatantly recruited and transported to the United States large numbers of unskilled and illiterate immigrants, chiefly from Eastern Europe—would undermine labor reforms of any type.

27. John Ryan, *A Living Wage: Its Ethical and Economic Aspects* (New York: Macmillan, 1906).

28. Its most germane passage reads, "Let it be granted, then, that as a rule workman and employer should make arrangements, and in particular should freely agree as to wages; nevertheless, there is a dictate of nature more imperious and more ancient than any bargain between man and man, that the remuneration must be enough to support the wage earner in *reasonable and frugal comfort*. If through necessity, or fear of a worse evil, the workman accepts harder conditions because an employer or contractor will give him no better, he is the victim of fraud and injustice."

29. The influence of this school of thought in a number of areas can be seen in, for instance, Richard Epstein, *Takings: Private Property and the Power of Eminent Domain* (Cambridge, Mass.: Harvard University Press, 1985); and Richard Posner, *The Economics of Justice* (Cambridge, Mass.: Harvard University Press, 1981). It has also migrated into political science under the name public choice theory, guided by such people as Vincent Ostrom, James Buchanan, and Gordon Tullock.

30. Milton Friedman, *Capitalism and Freedom* (Chicago: University of Chicago Press, 1962); Milton Friedman and Rose Friedman, *Free to Choose: A Personal Statement* (New York: Harcourt Brace Jovanovich, 1980).

31. Friedman, *Capitalism and Freedom*, 8.

32. Ibid., 12.

33. Friedman and Friedman, *Free to Choose*, 305.

34. For a discussion of this issue, see Robert Kuttner, *Everything for Sale: The Virtues and Limits of Markets* (New York: Knopf, 1997); and Cass Sunstein, *Free Markets and Social Justice* (New York: Oxford University Press, 1997). Although some of the essays are somewhat dated because they concentrate on Eastern European socialist societies of the day, the ideas found in John W. Chapman and J. Ronald Pennock, eds., *Markets and Justice* (New York: New York University Press, 1989), are worth perusing.

35. For a thorough analysis of testing models, see Adolph Lowe, *On Economic Knowledge: Toward a Science of Political Economics* (New York: Harper and Row, 1965).

36. Some moderate free market economists admit that the minimum wage has some potential positive effects, such as reducing income inequities; however, they contend the net result is still negative. I am speaking only of the hardcore free marketeers in the text.

37. Friedman, *Capitalism and Freedom*, 35, 180–81.

38. Rob Norton, "The Minimum Wage Is Unfair," *Fortune*, May 27, 1996, 53.

39. James Bovard, "How Fair Are the Fair Labor Standards?" *Regulation* 18 (1995): 67, 75.

40. The concept of collective goods is developed in Mancur Olson, *The Logic of Collective Action* (Cambridge, Mass.: Harvard University Press, 1965).

41. On the often neglected power of persuasive argument in Congress, see Joseph Bessette, *The Mild Voice of Reason: Deliberative Democracy and American National Government* (Chicago: University of Chicago Press, 1992).

42. Mickey Kaus, *The End of Equality* (New York: Basic Books, 1992).

43. Norman Furniss and Timothy Tilton, *The Case for the Welfare State* (Bloomington: Indiana University Press, 1977), 193–94.

44. B. Guy Peters, "The Limits of the Welfare State," in *Political Economy in Western Democracies,* ed. Norman Vig and Steven Schier (New York: Holmes and Meier, 1985), 91–114. My colleagues and I were just as guilty of neglect when we surveyed public policies in the United States and Britain about the same time. See Jerold Waltman and Donley Studlar, eds., *Political Economy: Public Policies in the United States and Britain* (Jackson: University Press of Mississippi, 1987).

45. "Greed Lives," *Progressive,* June 1996, 8–9.

46. Barry Bluestone and Teresa Ghilarducci, "Rewarding Work: A Feasible Antipoverty Policy," *American Prospect,* May–June 1996, 40–46.

47. Edward Irons, "Raise the Minimum Wage," *Black Enterprise,* December 1995, 28.

48. U.S. Congress, Joint Economic Committee, *Evidence against a Higher Minimum Wage: Hearings before the Joint Economic Committee,* part 1, 104th Cong., 1st sess., February 25, 1995, 40–45.

49. Michael Sandel, *Democracy's Discontent: America in Search of a Public Philosophy* (Cambridge, Mass.: Harvard University Press, 1996), 124.

50. The literature on civic republicanism is vast. In addition to Sandel, *Democracy's Discontent,* see Richard Sinopoli, *The Foundations of American Citizenship: Liberalism, the Constitution, and Civic Virtue* (New York: Oxford University Press, 1992); Robert Bellah, Richard Madsen, William Sullivan, Ann Swidler, and Steven Tipton, *Habits of the Heart: Individualism and Commitment in American Life* (Berkeley: University of California Press, 1985); Alan Ehrenhalt, *The Lost City: The Forgotten Virtues of Community in America* (New York: Basic Books, 1995); and Amatai Etzioni, *The Spirit of Community: Rights, Responsibilities, and the Communitarian Agenda* (New York: Crown, 1993).

51. Eisenach, *Lost Promise of Progressivism.* Most modern social welfare theory is based on a school known as welfare economics. For a survey, see

Hans van den Doel and Ben van Velthoven, *Democracy and Welfare Economics* (Cambridge: Cambridge University Press, 1993). An accessible discussion of the value assumptions underlying the approach can be found in Charles Rowley and Alan Peacock, *Welfare Economics: A Liberal Restatement* (New York: Wiley, 1975). The basic idea is that people have preferences that are not revealed in ordinary dispersed markets. If these preferences are accounted for, maximizing welfare, then the total welfare of society's members can be greater. At its most basic level, however, this model does not challenge the essentially economic character and the sanctity of individual preferences.

52. See, for example, Lawrence Mishel, Jared Bernstein, and Edith Rasell, *Who Wins with a Higher Minimum Wage* (Washington, D.C.: Economic Policy Institute, 1995).

Chapter 2: A Brief Political History through 1989

1. Quoted in James Hodges, *New Deal Labor Policy and the Southern Cotton Textile Industry, 1933–41* (Knoxville: University of Tennessee Press, 1986), 180.

2. The various state enactments are covered in Orme Phelps, *The Legislative Background of the Fair Labor Standards Act* (Chicago: University of Chicago Press, 1939).

3. Quoted in ibid., 55.

4. *Adkins v. Children's Hospital,* 261 U.S. 525 (1923).

5. *West Coast Hotel Co. v. Parrish,* 300 U.S. 379 (1937).

6. For an intensive study of the place of the minimum wage in the New Deal, see George Paulsen, *A Living Wage for the Forgotten Man: The Quest for Fair Labor Standards, 1933–41* (Selingsgrove, Pa.: Susquehanna University Press, 1996).

7. There are many works dealing with almost every aspect of the New Deal. The classic remains William E. Leuchtenburg, *Franklin D. Roosevelt and the New Deal* (New York: Harper, 1963). For an economic analysis, see Michael Bernstein, *The Great Depression: Delayed Recovery and Economic Change in America* (Cambridge: Cambridge University Press, 1987).

8. On the NIRA, see Bernard Bellush, *The Failure of the NRA* (New York: Norton, 1975).

9. These are drawn from M. D. Vincent and Beulah Amidon, "NRA: A Trial Balance," *Survey Graphic,* July 1935, 333–37, 363–64.

10. *Schechter Poultry Corporation v. U.S.,* 295 U.S. 495 (1935).

11. Quoted in Conrad Fritsch and Steven Connell, "Evolution of Wage and

Hours Laws in the United States," in United States, Minimum Wage Study Commission, *Report of the Minimum Wage Study Commission,* vol. 2 (Washington, D.C.: Government Printing Office, 1981), 17. The Minimum Wage Study Commission was established by Congress in 1977 to analyze the effects of the minimum wage and report to the president.

12. A brief history can be found in Bernard Schwartz, *A History of the Supreme Court* (New York: Oxford University Press, 1993), chaps. 7–9. Although it has a pointed normative flavor, Bernard Siegan's *Economic Liberties and the Constitution* (Chicago: University of Chicago Press, 1980) contains an in-depth analysis of the various doctrinal positions.

13. *National Labor Relations Board v. Jones and Laughlin Steel Corporation,* 301 U.S. 1 (1937). The intriguing history of this case is told in Richard Cortner, *The Jones and Laughlin Case* (New York: Knopf, 1970).

14. Quoted in Paul Douglas and Joseph Hackman, "The Fair Labor Standards Act, I," *Political Science Quarterly* 53 (1939): 493. This article and its companion piece in volume 54, pp. 29–55, of the same journal, are excellent contemporary analyses of the legislative history of the FLSA. A more recent study is Jonathan Grossman, "Fair Labor Standards Act of 1938: Maximum Struggle for a Minimum Wage," *Monthly Labor Review,* June 1978, 22–30.

15. There have always been two classes of workers not subject to the act: the "uncovered" workers and those "covered" workers who are "exempt" for some specific reason. Agricultural and retail workers have always been "covered," but they have been "exempt."

16. Quoted in Grossman, "Fair Labor Standards Act of 1938," 25.

17. Unions were lukewarm at best in their support for the FLSA, largely because they feared it might undermine collective bargaining. The last provision was inserted to allay those concerns.

18. The following capsule histories are based chiefly on the summaries provided in the annual *Congressional Quarterly Almanac* (Washington, D.C.: Congressional Quarterly) and the relevant chapters of Willis Nordlund, *The Quest for a Living Wage: A History of the Federal Minimum Wage Program* (Westport, Conn.: Greenwood, 1997). The *New York Times* and the *Washington Post,* of course, also carry daily stories on important political activity. To save countless footnotes, I provide citations only when there is a direct quote.

19. Statement of Maurice Tobin, the secretary of labor, and William McComb, the administrator of the Wage and Hour Division, quoted in *New York Times,* January 28, 1949.

20. These cases are noted in U.S. Congress, House of Representatives, *Con-*

ference Report on Fair Labor Standards Amendments of 1949, House Report No. 1453, 81st Cong., 1st sess., 2252–53.

21. *New York Times,* August 12, 1949.

22. Ibid., January 10, 1955.

23. Ibid., December 21, 1960.

24. *Congressional Quarterly Almanac, 1961,* 475.

25. Ibid., 482.

26. This meant, for example, that if an employee collected enough in tips to meet or exceed the minimum wage, he or she would be paid nothing. A tip credit of 50 percent would force all employers to pay these people this amount as a base.

27. *National League of Cities v. Usery,* 426 U.S. 833 (1976).

28. *Garcia v. San Antonio Metropolitan Transit Authority,* 469 U.S. 528 (1985).

29. Quoted in Nordlund, *Quest for a Living Wage,* 179, 180.

Chapter 3: Public Opinion

1. Gallup Poll, July 12, 1936. Polls are cited by the sponsoring organization and the release date, which is sometimes a few days or even weeks after the interview date(s). Some of these polls have been sponsored by groups with an interest in the minimum wage, but only those polls conducted by reputable polling organizations are included here. The national sample is adults unless otherwise noted. Most of these polls are archived at the Roper Center for Public Opinion Research at the University of Connecticut.

2. Gallup Poll, June 6, 1937.

3. Ibid., January 13, 1938.

4. Ibid., February 16, 1938.

5. Ibid., May 11, 1938.

6. Ibid., January 2, 1939.

7. See Robert Erikson, Norman Luttbeg, and Kent Tedin, *American Public Opinion,* 4th ed. (New York: Macmillan, 1991), 198–201.

8. Associated Press Poll, May 1996.

9. Interuniversity Consortium for Political and Social Research, University of Michigan, National Election Studies.

10. The "most important problem" surveys are reported periodically in the *Gallup Poll Monthly.*

11. CBS News/*New York Times* Poll, April 16, 1989.

12. Tarrance Group, April 4, 1995.

13. CBS News Poll, October 1, 1996.

14. *Newsweek* Poll, August 23, 1996.

15. NBC News/*Wall Street Journal* Poll, September 17, 1996.

16. For a careful analysis of the conceptual and logistical problems of polling in general, see Herbert Asher, *Polling and the Public: What Every Citizen Should Know,* 3d ed. (Washington, D.C.: Congressional Quarterly Press, 1995).

17. CNN/*USA Today* Poll, April 10, 1996.

18. NBC News/*Wall Street Journal* Poll, April 4, 1995.

19. ABC News/*Washington Post* Poll, April 3, 1989.

20. Democratic Leadership Council, November 17, 1994.

21. *Los Angeles Times* Poll, January 26, 1995.

22. ABC News/*Washington Post* Poll, April 3, 1989.

23. CNN/*USA Today* Poll, May 12, 1996.

24. NBC News/Microsoft Poll, July 15, 1996.

25. Associated Press Poll, April 30, 1996.

26. NBC News/*Wall Street Journal* Poll, May 15, 1996.

27. Princeton Survey Research Associates, September 29, 1996.

28. *U.S. News and World Report* Poll, June 3, 1996.

29. *Los Angeles Times* Poll, August 6, 1996; *Newsweek* Poll, August 23, 1996.

30. Gallup Poll, January 13, 1997.

31. Gallup/American Institute of Public Opinion Poll, August 19, 1945.

32. Ibid., January 22, 1947, and May 28, 1947.

33. Ibid., December 1, 1948.

34. Roper Poll, June 1977; Gallup/American Institute of Public Opinion Poll, January 12, 1981; Hearst Poll, August 9, 1984; Service Employees International Union, May 25, 1987; Pew Research Center, May 13, 1996.

35. Service Employees International Union, May 25, 1987.

36. NBC News/*Wall Street Journal* Poll, August 8, 1996.

37. Ibid., May 15, 1996.

38. *Times-Mirror* Poll, March 21, 1994.

39. NBC News/*Wall Street Journal* Poll, January 18, 1994.

40. Associated Press Poll, May 1996.

41. Gallup Poll, May 10, 1992.

42. *Time*/CNN Poll, March 12, 1992.

43. NBC News/*Wall Street Journal* Poll, May 15, 1996.

44. J. R. Kearl, Clayne Pope, Gordon Whiting, and Larry Wimmer, "What Economists Think: A Confusion of Economists?" *American Economic Review* 69 (1978): 28–35. The actual statement was, "A minimum wage increases

unemployment among young and unskilled workers," with the choices of "generally agree," "agree with provisions," and "generally disagree." Sixty-eight percent opted for the first choice and 22 percent the second.

45. NBC News/*Wall Street Journal* Poll, May 15, 1996.

46. Princeton Survey Research Associates, June 30, 1993.

47. Harris Poll, April 1, 1996.

48. Associated Press Poll, May 1996.

49. *Los Angeles Times* Poll, March 25, 1981.

50. Roper Polls, April 1979 and April 1981.

51. Roper Report, November 1980.

52. Service Employees International Union, May 25, 1987.

53. Fox News Poll, October 30, 1996 (8 percent); Associated Press Poll, May 1996 (17 percent); ABC News/*Washington Post* Poll, April 3, 1989 (20 percent, with 8 percent reporting the minimum wage worker was the "chief wage earner" and 12 reporting "someone else" was).

The disparities can be partially explained by differences in sampling and wording of the questions. In the Fox News Poll, the sample was restricted to likely voters, whereas the other two drew on a national adult sample. Because many minimum wage workers are by definition low-income earners, statistically they are less likely to vote than the general population. The question asked if the respondent or anyone in the "household" was affected by the October 1, 1996, minimum wage increase.

The Associated Press Poll's question was, "Does someone in your immediate family earn just the minimum wage?" The ABC News/*Washington Post* Poll asked, "Would your salary or anyone in your immediate family's salary go up if" the minimum wage were to go up? This question would capture many people working above the minimum wage who believe an increase would push up their own earnings. The same thing would have happened with the question from the Fox News Poll.

In sum: (1) the sample was less inclusive in the Fox poll; (2) "household" and "immediate family" reach different groups of people; and (3) people would be included in the Fox and ABC/*Washington Post* polls who would not be in the Associated Press poll, since the Associated Press poll restricted itself to those at "just" the minimum wage.

54. Gallup Poll, December 13, 1960.

55. ABC News/*Washington Post* Poll, April 3, 1989; ABC News/*Washington Post* Poll, June 19, 1989; Associated Press Poll, July 16, 1989.

56. Center for the Study of Policy Priorities/Americans Talk Issues Foundation, December 8, 1994.

57. CNN/*USA Today* Poll, May 12, 1996.

58. The Gallup Poll asked people in 1948, "What would you say the minimum wage per hour should be today for a single person, just graduated from high school, and starting out at a beginner's job in a factory in this area?" Fifty-three percent chose seventy-five cents an hour and above, when the minimum wage stood at forty cents per hour.

59. Harris Poll, April 1, 1996; *New York Times* Poll, June 1996.

60. Service Employees International Union, May 25, 1987.

61. *Parents Magazine* Poll, May 15, 1989. In 1996, this would have required a minimum wage of $7.50 per hour.

62. Service Employees International Union, May 25, 1987.

63. Center for Survey Research, University of Virginia, April 14, 1996.

64. NBC News/*Wall Street Journal* Poll, May 15, 1996.

65. Ibid.

66. Associated Press Poll, May 1996.

67. ABC News/*Washington Post* Poll, April 3, 1989.

68. Center for the Study of Policy Attitudes/Americans Talk Issues Foundation, December 8, 1994.

69. MS Fund for Women/Center for Policy Alternatives, June 8, 1992.

70. CBS News/*New York Times* Poll, April 2, 1996 (emphasis added).

71. CNN/*USA Today* Poll, May 12, 1996 (emphasis added).

Chapter 4: The Sociology of the Minimum Wage

1. U.S. Department of Labor, Bureau of Labor Statistics, *Current Population Survey*, quarterly.

2. The problems are (1) piece rate workers are not included, since the question asks for only hourly rates; (2) tipped workers may or may not be included, especially since the "tip credit" comes into play (see pages 97–98); and (3) we do not know whether the people who report earning the minimum wage are covered by the Fair Labor Standards Act. That is, several small categories of workers are exempt, and the Current Population Survey reports only hourly pay.

3. All percentages are rounded to whole numbers, unless there is something to be gained by including decimals. The detail lost by doing this is outweighed by the need to keep things relatively clear and simple, since there are so many percentages used.

4. The Department of Labor defines full time as employment usually for 35 hours or more a week.

5. These figures, it is worth stressing, are people working at the prevailing minimum wage, at the time $4.75 per hour, and do not include all those affected by the increase to $5.15.

6. For a good analysis of women's participation in the labor force, see Alice Abel Kemp, *Women's Work: Degraded and Devalued* (Englewood Cliffs, N.J.: Prentice-Hall, 1994), chap. 6. See also Barbara Ann Stolz, *Still Struggling: America's Low-Income Working Women Confronting the 1980s* (Lexington, Mass.: D.C. Heath, 1985).

7. The number probably drops between ages 20 and 24, but that cannot be deduced from the data.

8. Unfortunately, the Bureau of Labor Statistics does not calculate the part-time and full-time status of minimum wage workers by age.

9. The gender breakdowns collapse retail and wholesale trade into one category. Since the wholesale numbers are quite small, these figures are roughly comparable with the retail figures in the previous paragraph.

10. Mexican origin; Puerto Rican origin; Cuban origin; Central and South American origin; and other Spanish. Eighty-six percent of Hispanic minimum wage workers classify themselves as of "Mexican origin."

11. Associated Press Poll, May 1996.

12. There are two that are referred to as "dedicated." One is assigned solely to vocational rehabilitation clients, the other to veterans.

13. The population of Forrest and Lamar counties, the major service area for this office, is 24 percent African American.

Chapter 5: Policy-Making

1. The narrative that follows is drawn from accounts in the *Congressional Quarterly Weekly Report,* the *New York Times,* the *Washington Post,* and Robert Reich's memoir *Locked in the Cabinet* (New York: Knopf, 1997). I have included specific notes only when a direct quote or important bit of factual information is referenced.

2. *Wall Street Journal,* August 12, 1993.

3. Reich, *Locked in the Cabinet,* 195.

4. The text of the speech is reprinted in the *New York Times,* January 25, 1996. The president's reference to the bipartisan nature of raising the minimum wage, constantly repeated by Democrats throughout the debate, was a bit disingenuous. Although the final, compromise-laden bill has often, as in 1989, had bipartisan support, the issue has hardly been one characterized by a bipartisan consensus.

5. Reich, *Locked in the Cabinet*, 237.

6. Quoted in *New York Times*, February 4, 1995.

7. Quoted in Reich, *Locked in the Cabinet*, 232–33.

8. U.S. Congress, Joint Economic Committee, *Evidence against a Higher Minimum Wage*, part 1, February 22, 1995.

9. Ibid., 86.

10. U.S. Congress, Senate Committee on Labor and Human Resources, *Examining Proposed Legislation to Increase the Federal Minimum Wage: Hearings before the Senate Committee on Labor and Human Resources*, 104th Cong., 1st sess., December 15, 1995.

11. An overview of the Senate's rules can be found in Roger Davidson and Walter Oleszek, *Congress and Its Members*, 6th ed. (Washington, D.C.: Congressional Quarterly Press, 1998), 229–46.

12. On the filibuster, see Sarah Binder and Steven Smith, *Politics or Principle: Filibustering in the United States Senate* (Washington, D.C.: Brookings Institution, 1996).

13. Quoted in *New York Times*, March 27, 1996.

14. Quoted in *Washington Post*, March 27, 1996.

15. Quoted in *New York Times*, March 27, 1996.

16. They were James Jeffords from Vermont, Arlen Specter from Pennsylvania, Alphonse D'Amato from New York, and Mark Hatfield from Oregon.

17. This means four additional Republicans voted with the Democrats. However, that does not mean all of them would have voted for the minimum wage increase itself. They could have only wanted to dispense with the issue once and for all.

18. Quoted in *New York Times*, March 29, 1996.

19. It is generally much harder for a minority to force action in the House than in the Senate. The rules in the House are designed to give the majority levers to get its own bills passed. See Davidson and Oleszek, *Congress and Its Members*, 229–39.

20. Quoted in *Washington Post*, April 19, 1996.

21. Ibid., April 24, 1996.

22. Ibid., April 26, 1996.

23. Quoted in *New York Times*, April 18, 1996.

24. Quoted in *Washington Post*, May 8, 1996.

25. Quoted in ibid., April 25, 1996.

26. Clinton worked this angle masterfully on, for example, the flood relief bill in 1996, to which Republicans tried to attach riders involving future government shutdowns and the census.

27. Actually, it was a four-point package, but one dealt with computer consultants who worked at high multiples of the minimum wage and is therefore marginal to our concerns. Keep in mind that the tax cut bill would be voted on separately.

28. Jonathan Weisman, "Senate May Reprise 1989 Fight over 'Training Wage,'" *Congressional Quarterly Weekly Report,* June 8, 1996, 1600–1601.

29. While the House Rules Committee no longer has the power to bottle up legislation on substantive grounds that it had in the 1930s, it still maintains control over the House calendar. As it did here by dividing the bills, structuring votes can be quite important.

30. *Congressional Quarterly Weekly Report,* May 25, 1996, 1461–62.

31. The debate is in *Congressional Record,* May 23, 1996.

32. The figure was based on fifty weeks of employment per year. Using fifty-two weeks, it comes to $8,840.

33. David Card and Alan Krueger, *Myth and Measurement: The New Economics of the Minimum Wage* (Princeton, N.J.: Princeton University Press, 1995).

34. How he derived that figure was not specified.

35. It involved payment for employees' commuting time.

36. One reason the tax portion of the bill grew is that many senators were convinced that this was the only tax bill likely to pass this session; hence, it was now or never for their pet projects, which were never in short supply.

37. The literature on policy-making is vast. Three good introductions are Charles O. Jones, *An Introduction to the Study of Public Policy,* 3d ed. (Monterey, Calif.: Brooks/Cole, 1984); Randall Ripley and Grace Franklin, *Congress, the Bureaucracy, and Public Policy,* 5th ed. (New York: Harcourt Brace, 1990); and Charles E. Lindblom and Edward Woodhouse, *The Policy-Making Process,* 3d ed. (Englewood Cliffs, N.J.: Prentice-Hall, 1993).

38. The literature is voluminous. A good survey of traditional and recent processes is Barbara Sinclair, *Unorthodox Lawmaking: New Legislative Processes in the U.S. Congress* (Washington, D.C.: Congressional Quarterly Press, 1997).

39. See, for example, Nordlund, *Quest for a Living Wage.*

40. Roger Cobb and Charles Elder, *Participation in American Politics: The Dynamics of Agenda Building* (Baltimore: Johns Hopkins University Press, 1972). The more important works are Robert Eyestone, *From Social Issues to Public Policy* (New York: Wiley, 1978); John Kingdon, *Issues, Alternatives, and Public Policy* (Boston: Little, Brown, 1984); Frank Baumgartner and Bryan Jones, *Agendas and Instability in American Politics* (Chicago: University of

Chicago Press, 1993); and David Rochefort and Roger Cobb, eds., *The Politics of Problem Definition* (Lawrence: University Press of Kansas, 1994).

41. Most of the work on agenda building to date has focused on how issues initially move from matters of social concern to items being discussed by governmental decision makers. Little attention has been given to such recurring issues as minimum wage increases.

42. Although William Schiller does not discuss the minimum wage, his article "Senators as Political Entrepreneurs: Using Bill Sponsoring to Shape Legislative Agendas," *American Journal of Political Science* 39 (1995): 186–203, provides some interesting data on the volume of bills introduced. In a typical session, 3,000 bills are introduced in the Senate alone.

Chapter 6: Impact and Feedback

1. These are discussed in Nordlund, *Quest for a Living Wage,* passim.

2. United States, Minimum Wage Study Commission, *Report of the Minimum Wage Study Commission.*

3. For a succinct discussion of Congress's relationship with interest groups, see Davidson and Oleszek, *Congress and Its Members,* chap. 12.

4. On access, see Leroy Rieselbach, *Congressional Politics: The Evolving Legislative System,* 2d ed. (Boulder, Colo.: Westview, 1995), 237–39.

5. U.S. Department of Commerce, *Statistical Abstract of the United States, 1996* (Washington, D.C.: Government Printing Office, 1997). On turnout in American elections, see William Keefe, *Parties, Politics, and Public Policy in America,* 8th ed. (Washington, D.C.: Congressional Quarterly Press, 1998), 172–83, especially table 5-3; John Bibby, *Politics, Parties, and Elections in America,* 3d ed. (Chicago: Nelson Hall, 1996), 254–63; and M. Margaret Conway, *Political Participation in the United States,* 2d ed. (Washington, D.C.: Congressional Quarterly Press, 1991).

6. Card and Krueger, *Myth and Measurement,* 396.

7. Sar Levitan and Richard Belous, *More Than Subsistence: Minimum Wages for the Working Poor* (Baltimore: Johns Hopkins University Press, 1979), 126.

8. R. H. Tawney, *The Establishment of Minimum Wages in the Chain Making Industry under the Trade Board Act of 1909* (London: Bell, 1914), xi.

9. Any standard textbook in labor economics contains an explanation of this, but a particularly readable one is Ronald Ehrenberg and Robert Smith, *Modern Labor Economics: Theory and Public Policy,* 4th ed. (New York: Harper Collins, 1994), chaps. 2 and 3.

10. It also assumes that every worker has perfect information about all openings.

11. The usual convention in economics writings is to begin the initial point with a 0 subscript. I think clarity will be enhanced if we use 1 and 2 here.

12. A vigorous explication and defense of the conventional model can be found in Gary Becker, "It's Simple: Hike the Minimum Wage and You Put People out of Work," *Business Week*, March 6, 1995, 22. For more detailed treatments, see D. Eric Schansberg, *Poor Policy: How Government Harms the Poor* (Boulder, Colo.: Westview, 1996), chap. 6; and Richard B. McKenzie, *Times Change: The Minimum Wage and the New York Times* (San Francisco: Pacific Research Institute for Public Policy, 1994).

13. Finis Welch, *Minimum Wages: Issues and Evidence* (Washington, D.C.: American Enterprise Institute, 1978), 1.

14. This assumes a given level of capital goods, such as plant and equipment.

15. The clothing study is R. H. Tawney, *The Establishment of Minimum Wages in the Tailoring Industry under the Trade Board Act of 1909* (London: Bell, 1915).

16. Tawney, *The Establishment of Minimum Wages in the Chain Making Industry*, 105.

17. Richard Lester, "Shortcomings of Marginal Analysis for Wage-Employment Problems," *American Economic Review* 36 (1946): 63–82.

18. George Stigler, "The Economics of Minimum Wage Legislation," *American Economic Review* 36 (1946): 361. It is also informative to look at the exchange between Lester and Stigler that followed. See Richard Lester, "Marginalism, Minimum Wages, and Labor Markets," *American Economic Review* 37 (1947): 135–48; and George Stigler, "Professor Lester and the Marginalists," *American Economic Review* 37 (1947): 154–57.

19. There were steep recessions in both those years.

20. This does not address whether there may be a political factor, namely, that Congress enacts minimum wage increases only during good times. This is discussed in Madeline Zavodny, "The Minimum Wage: Maximum Controversy over a Minimal Effect?" (Ph.D. diss., Massachusetts Institute of Technology, 1996), chap. 2.

21. Charles Brown, Curtis Gilroy, and Andrew Kohen, "The Effect of the Minimum Wage on Employment and Unemployment," *Journal of Economic Literature* 20 (1982): 508.

22. Walter Wessels, *Minimum Wages, Fringe Benefits, and Working Con-*

ditions (Washington, D.C.: American Enterprise Institute, 1980); Masanori Hashimoto, "Minimum Wage Effects on Training on the Job," *American Economic Review* 72 (1982): 1070–87.

23. U.S. Congress, Joint Economic Committee, *Evidence against a Higher Minimum Wage,* part 2, April 5, 1995, 49.

24. Allison Wellington, "Effects of the Minimum Wage on the Employment Status of Youths: An Update," *Journal of Human Resources* 26 (1991): 27–46.

25. The best-known studies utilizing this approach are David Neumark and William Wascher, "Employment Effects of Minimum Wages and Subminimum Wages: Panel Data on State Minimum Wage Laws," *Industrial and Labor Relations Review* 46 (1992): 55–81; and Nicolas Williams, "Regional Effects of the Minimum Wage on Teenage Employment," *Applied Economics* 25 (1993): 1517–28.

26. See, among others, Peter Linneman, "The Economic Impacts of Minimum Wage Laws: A New Look at an Old Question," *Journal of Political Economy* 90 (1982): 443–69; and William Rodgers, "The Minimum Wage and Racial Differences in Teenage Unemployment" (Department of Economics, College of William and Mary, 1995).

27. Taiel Kim and Lowell Taylor, "The Employment Effect in Retail Trade of California's 1988 Minimum Wage Increase," *Journal of Business and Economic Statistics* 13 (1995): 175–82.

28. Kim and Taylor used *County Business Patterns,* a series published by the Department of Commerce. Its chief shortcoming is that it does not contain information on hourly wages; hence, the analyst must make estimates to create employment figures. See the discussion in Card and Krueger, *Myth and Measurement,* 101–8.

29. Lawrence Katz and Alan Krueger, "The Effect of the Minimum Wage on the Fast Food Industry," *Industrial and Labor Relations Review* 46 (1992): 6–21.

30. U.S. Congress, Joint Economic Committee, *Evidence against a Higher Minimum Wage,* part 2, April 5, 1995.

31. There are some instances in psychology and education where it can be approximated, although in psychological studies, serious ethical issues can arise regarding informing people about the nature of what is going on.

32. Many of the critics have essays in Marvin Kosters, ed., *The Employment Effects of Minimum Wages* (Washington, D.C.: American Enterprise Institute, 1996). This volume resulted from a conference on the book. (If perusing this book, be certain to read the letter from Card and Krueger in the preface.) Three of the severest critics, Donald Deere, Kevin Murphy, and Fi-

nis Welch, wrote a piece entitled "Sense and Nonsense on the Minimum Wage" in *Regulation* 18 (1995): 47–56. The most enlightening comments are contained in a symposium on the book published in the *Industrial and Labor Relations Review* 48 (1995): 827–49.

33. Comments in the symposium, *Industrial and Labor Relations Review,* 832.

34. Zavodny, "Minimum Wage."

35. All textbooks on labor economics have a discussion of this model. Ehrenberg and Smith, *Modern Labor Economics,* is particularly clear.

36. These are discussed in Nordlund, *Quest for a Living Wage,* passim.

37. United States, Minimum Wage Study Commission, *Report of the Minimum Wage Study Commission,* vol. 1, chap. 3, contains a summary of the research on inflation. The more detailed studies are in vol. 6. See also the article by one of the lead researchers, Brigitte Sellekaerts, "The Effect of the Minimum Wage on Inflation and Other Key Macroeconomic Variables," *Eastern Economics Journal* 3 (1982): 177–90.

38. United States, Minimum Wage Study Commission, *Report of the Minimum Wage Study Commission,* vol. 1, 69.

39. This is assuming, of course, that the price increase of the goods and services they purchase is under 10.0 percent. The 0.3 figure applies to all prices, including fur coats, first-class airfares, and BMWs, all of which are irrelevant to most minimum wage workers. It seems highly unlikely, though, that with only a 0.3 percent rise overall, goods and services consumed by the typical minimum wage worker would go up by anything near 10.0 percent.

40. William Alpert, *The Minimum Wage in the Restaurant Industry* (New York: Praeger, 1986), 53.

41. Ibid., 95.

42. Card and Krueger, *Myth and Measurement,* 52–56.

43. Zavodny, "Minimum Wage," 36–39.

44. Gross profit is the difference between the selling price and the cost to produce or buy the good. It does not include selling and administrative expenses, the subtraction of which from gross profit leaves net income.

45. U.S. Congress, Joint Economic Committee, *Evidence against a Higher Minimum Wage,* part 1, February 22, 1995, 22.

46. Alpert, *Minimum Wage in the Restaurant Industry,* 93.

47. Card and Krueger, *Myth and Measurement,* chap. 10.

48. Ibid., 347–48. They also found that McDonalds did not modify its expansion program when the minimum wage increased.

49. Jerold Waltman, Allan McBride, and Nicole Camhout, "Minimum Wage

Increases and the Business Failure Rate," *Journal of Economic Issues* 32 (1998): 219–23. We confined our analyses to this period because Dun and Bradstreet changed the way it computes the failure rate in 1984, making later data not wholly comparable with those from the earlier years.

50. Zavodny, "Minimum Wage," 40.

51. It is interesting that there has been virtually no research on the role of the minimum wage in purchasing power and business profits, especially since that was one of the reasons Franklin D. Roosevelt gave for the program in the first place.

52. Donald Parsons, *Poverty and the Minimum Wage* (Washington, D.C.: American Enterprise Institute, 1980), 62.

53. Ronald Mincy, "Raising the Minimum Wage: Effects on Family Poverty," *Monthly Labor Review*, July 1990, 18–25.

54. Card and Krueger, *Myth and Measurement*, 307. Richard Burkhauser, Kenneth Couch, and David Wittenberg contended this estimate was too high. See their article "Who Gets What from Minimum Wage Hikes: A Re-Estimation of Card and Krueger's Distributional Analysis in *Myth and Measurement: The New Economics of the Minimum Wage*," *Industrial and Labor Relations Review* 49 (1996): 547–52.

55. Deborah Figart and June Lapidus, "A Gender Analysis of Labor Market Policies for the Working Poor," *Feminist Economics* 1 (1995): 1–22.

56. That people express concern about unemployment even if they themselves face no chance of being laid off contributes to the argument that the American public is, at least partly, imbued with civic republican ideals. As Michael Lewis-Beck and Tom Rice, two noted students of American public opinion, have written, "The overwhelming evidence is that American voters hardly respond to their pocketbooks; instead they seem to care mostly about the nation's economic well-being." Quoted in *Congressional Quarterly Weekly Report*, July 25, 1992, 2153.

57. A political scientist's first suspicion is that these programs get more attention than the minimum wage because they involve governmental budgets and are administered by large bureaucracies, staffed mostly by middle-class people. In contrast, the minimum wage involves no public expenditures and its enforcement is in the hands of a small agency with few personnel.

Conclusion

1. Hart, *Bound by Our Constitution*.

2. Smith, *Comparative Policy Process*, 90.

3. Frances Perkins's account of the administration's internal debates over the Social Security bill, both the old age pension and unemployment insurance aspects of the measure, for example, demonstrates this clearly. See Frances Perkins, *The Roosevelt I Knew* (New York: Harpers, 1946).

4. A number of recent books on the nature of work are discussed in Alan Wolfe's review essay, "The Moral Meanings of Work," *American Prospect*, September–October 1997, 82–90. One of the best analyses of the public's views on the value of work is Steven Teles, *Whose Welfare? AFDC and Elite Politics* (Lawrence: University Press of Kansas, 1996), chap. 3.

5. An excellent study of Jeffersonian political economy is Lance Banning, *The Jeffersonian Persuasion: Evolution of a Party Ideology* (Ithaca, N.Y.: Cornell University Press, 1978).

6. The best discussion of the need for this space and its diminution in modern America is Kaus, *End of Equality*.

7. For the most thorough analysis, see Sandel, *Democracy's Discontent*.

8. Nancy Fraser, *Justice Interruptus: Critical Reflections on the "Postsocialist" Condition* (New York: Routledge: 1997), chap. 2.

9. Ibid., 50.

10. Lawrence Mead, *Beyond Entitlement: The Social Obligations of Citizenship* (New York: Free Press, 1986). The rise of paternalism is discussed in his article "Telling the Poor What to Do," *Public Interest*, Summer 1998, 97–112, and in his essays "The Rise of Paternalism" and "Welfare Employment," in *The New Paternalism: Supervisory Approaches to Poverty*, ed. Lawrence Mead (Washington, D.C.: Brookings Institution, 1997), 1–38 and 39–88.

11. James Q. Wilson, "Paternalism, Democracy, and Bureaucracy," in *New Paternalism*, ed. Mead, 330–43.

12. E. J. Dionne, *Why Americans Hate Politics* (New York: Simon and Schuster, 1991), 333.

INDEX

AFDC. *See* Aid to Families with Dependent Children
African Americans, 62; and the minimum wage, 23, 51, 53; as minimum wage workers, 70, 71, 72, 73–74, 75, 83, 87. *See also* Minorities
Age: of minimum wage workers, 71–73, 83–85; and support for the minimum wage, 53. *See also* Teenagers
Agendas. *See* Political agendas
Agricultural exemption, 34, 40, 41
Aid to Families with Dependent Children (AFDC), 23, 132. *See also* Welfare
Alpert, William, 125, 127
American Enterprise Institute, 17
American Prospect (magazine), 23
Anderson, James L., 3
Andrews, John B., 13, 16
Armey, Dick, 91, 95
Australia, 11, 14, 16, 29, 142

Belous, Richard, 111
Bennett, Robert, 91
Black Enterprise (magazine), 23–24
Bluestone, Barry, 23
Bond, Christopher, 103
Bonior, David, 95
Bovard, James, 20

Britain. *See* United Kingdom
Brookings Institution, 21
Brown, Charles, 118, 130
Buchanan, Pat, 92
Burtless, Gary, 118
Bush, George, 44, 45, 46, 47, 54, 107
Business failures, 15–16, 101, 126–28, 132, 137, 145

Cain, Herman, 126
Card, David, 100, 119, 120–23, 125, 127–28, 130–31
Carter, Jimmy, 43–44
Cato Institute, 17
Center for Budget and Policy Priorities, 21
"Chicago school," 18. *See also* Free market fundamentalism
Christoph, James B., 3
Citizenship, 1, 10, 24–27, 48–49, 68, 140–45
Civic republicanism, 10, 25, 62, 68, 141–45
Classical economics, 13
Clinton, Bill, 54, 57, 58, 89–92, 94, 96–97, 99, 104, 106–7
Cobb, Roger, 105
Commons, John R., 13, 16
Congress, 5, 6, 17, 20, 21, 22, 30, 32,

33, 36, 38, 43, 49, 54–58, 63, 64,
89–104, 106, 108–10, 122, 124, 133,
135–36, 140. *See also* House of Representatives; Senate
Croly, Herbert, 16

Daschle, Tom, 93, 94, 102, 106–7
Daynes, Byron, 5
DeLay, Tom, 101
Democratic party. *See* Democrats
Democrats, 35, 36, 38, 39, 42–46, 53,
85, 90, 91, 93–99, 102–4, 106, 107,
140–41
Department of Labor, 35, 78, 98, 107,
108, 130
Dionne, E. J., 145
Dole, Bob, 57, 89, 92–97, 102
Dole, Elizabeth, 44

Earned Income Tax Credit, 23, 95
Economic inequality, 21, 24, 26–27, 143
Economic Policy Institute, 21
Education: and support for the mini-
mum wage, 51
Eisenach, Eldon, 13, 27
Eisenhower, Dwight D., 36–38
Elder, Charles, 105
Ely, Richard T., 14
Employment. *See* Unemployment

Fair Labor Standards Act, 20, 24, 28,
32–34, 48, 96, 98–99, 130, 135
Figart, Deborah, 131
Fine, Sidney, 14
Frankfurter, Felix, 12
Fraser, Nancy, 144
Freeman, Richard, 121
Free market fundamentalism, 17–19
Free market fundamentalists, 18–20,
139
Friedman, Milton, 18, 19
Furniss, Norman, 22

Gephardt, Dick, 94, 100
Ghilarducci, Teresa, 23
Gilroy, Curtis, 118, 130

Gingrich, Newt, 91, 95, 96, 97
Goodling, William, 97–99
Gore, Al, 103
Groat, George, 16

Harrison, Simon, 4, 137–38
Hart, Vivien, 135
Heritage Foundation, 17
Hispanics, 51, 70, 81–82, 83. *See also*
Minorities
Holcombe, Arthur, 15, 16
House of Representatives, 33–34, 37–
38, 41, 42, 43, 45, 46, 94, 95, 97–
102, 104
House Rules Committee, 33, 98
Hutchinson, Tim, 101

Income: and support for the minimum
wage, 51
Indexing, 35, 43, 45, 60
Inflation, 16, 23, 35, 40–42, 49, 66, 99,
101, 123–26, 132, 137, 139, 145
Irons, Edward, 24

James, William, 13
Jeffersonian thought, 142
Johnson, Lyndon, 39–41

Katz, Lawrence, 119
Kaus, Mickey, 21
Kellow, Aynsely, 4, 5
Kennedy, John F., 37, 38–39
Kennedy, Ted, 93, 102–3, 104, 106
Kim, Taiel, 119, 121
King, Peter, 95
Kloppenberg, James, 13
Kohen, Andrew, 118, 130
Krueger, Alan, 100, 119, 120–23, 125,
127–28, 130–31

Labor markets, 18, 20, 111–15
Labor unions. *See* Unions
Lapidus, June, 131
Laveleye, Emile de, 14
Leo XIII (pope), 17
Lester, Richard, 115

Levitan, Sar, 111
Liberals. *See* Social welfare liberals
Living wage, 17, 64
Lott, Trent, 89, 102
Lowi, Theodore, J., 1–5, 137

Malthus, Thomas, 13
Massachusetts minimum wage law, 10, 11, 12, 28, 141
Maximum hours, 28, 35, 96, 103. *See also* Fair Labor Standards Act
Mead, Lawrence, 144
MESC. *See* Mississippi Employment Security Commission
Mincy, Ronald, 130
Minimum wage laws. *See* Massachusetts minimum wage law; State minimum wage laws
Minimum Wage Study Commission, 108–9, 124–25, 126
Minimum wage workers, 60, 61, 67–68, 69–88, 104, 118–19, 133, 137. *See also* African Americans; Age; Women
Minorities, 43, 60, 61, 101–2, 109, 118, 119. *See also* African Americans; Hispanics
Mississippi Employment Security Commission (MESC), 85–87
Mitchell, James, 36, 37
Monopsony, 122–23
Monthly Labor Review (magazine), 106
Motley, John, 103

National Consumers' League (NCL), 11–12
National Federation of Independent Businesses, 91, 95
National Industrial Recovery Act (NIRA), 30–31, 135
National Recovery Administration (NRA). *See* National Industrial Recovery Act
NCL. *See* National Consumers' League
Neoclassical economics, 18, 126, 127, 136, 141. *See also* Free market fundamentalism

New Deal, 10, 21, 28, 30, 49, 132, 141
New Zealand, 11, 16
Nickles, Don, 102, 104
NIRA. *See* National Industrial Recovery Act
Nixon, Richard, 38, 41–42
Norton, Rob, 19
NRA. *See* National Recovery Administration

O'Neil, Tip, 43
Organized labor. *See* Unions

Panetta, Leon, 90, 91
Parsons, Donald, 129–30
Pepper, Claude, 33
Peters, B. Guy, 22
Policy: classification of, 1–6, 137–40; definition of, 3–5. *See also* Symbolic policy
Political agendas, 23, 104–7, 110, 136, 142
Political economy of citizenship. *See* Citizenship
Populists, 12
Poverty, 21, 39, 40, 80, 99–100, 110, 129–32, 141
Progressive (magazine), 22–23
Progressives, 10–11, 12–14, 15–17, 27, 132, 135, 141
Progressivism, 10–17, 145
Public opinion, 48–68, 144–45; influence on politics, 6, 135–36, 138–40, 145

Radanovich, George, 102
Reagan, Ronald, 44, 109
Reich, Robert, 89, 90, 91–92, 99, 103, 106, 123
Republican party. *See* Republicans
Republicans, 34–35, 36, 39, 40–42, 44–46, 53, 85, 89, 91, 93–98, 100–104, 140–41
Retail exemption, 34, 37, 39, 40, 41, 43, 44, 45
Ricardo, David, 13

"Ripple effect," 24, 124, 129, 131
Roosevelt, Franklin D., 28, 29, 32, 49,
    135
Roosevelt, Teddy, 30
Rubin, Robert, 90
Ryan, John, 17

Sandel, Michael, 24–25
Saxton, James, 91–92
Schattschneider, E. E., 4
Senate, 32–33, 36–37, 38, 40, 41, 42,
    43, 45, 92–95, 97, 102–4, 105
Shadegg, John, 101
Shays, Christopher, 100
Small business exemption, 44–45, 46,
    47, 98–99, 103. See also Retail ex-
    emption
Smith, Adam, 13
Smith, T. Alexander, 3, 6, 138, 139
Social Gospel, 13
Social welfare liberals, 9, 10, 21–23, 27,
    40, 132, 141–43
Souder, Mark, 101
Spitzer, Robert, 2, 3
State minimum wage laws, 11, 15, 28–
    30, 135. See also Massachusetts mini-
    mum wage law
State of the Union addresses, 34, 36,
    56–57, 90, 93
Stigler, George, 115
Subminimum wage. See Training wage
Supreme Court, 12, 29, 30, 31, 42, 49
Sweatshops, 11, 98, 141
Symbolic policy, 4, 17, 20, 137–40
Symbolic politics, 3, 6, 7, 69, 137–40.
    See also Symbolism
Symbolism, 1, 5, 17, 23, 24, 51, 53–54,
    98, 133, 136. See also Symbolic poli-
    tics

Tatalovich, Raymond, 5
Tawney, R. H., 111, 113, 121, 123, 124
Taylor, Lowell, 119, 121
Teenagers, 22, 61–62, 70, 83, 99, 101,
    110, 117–18. See also Age
Tilton, Timothy, 22
Tip credit, 41, 43, 44, 97
Training wage, 41, 42, 43, 44–46, 97,
    103
Truman, Harry, 24, 34–35

Unemployment, 15, 16–17, 59–62, 67,
    91, 101, 111–23, 132, 136–37, 145
Unions, 15, 24, 34, 38–39, 40, 41, 43,
    44, 45, 90, 94, 96, 103, 109, 135,
    136
United Kingdom, 7, 111

Victoria, Australia. See Australia

Wałęsa, Lech, 45
Wall Street Journal, 23, 89
Welch, Finis, 113
Welfare, 60, 100, 129, 131–32, 143–45.
    See also Aid to Families with Depen-
    dent Children
Wellington, Allison, 119
Williams, Pat, 95
Wilson, James Q., 144
Women: covered in early laws, 11–12,
    15, 28; as minimum wage workers,
    71–78, 83, 87, 99; organizations of,
    23, 24, 45, 109, 136; and support for
    the minimum wage, 51, 63, 67
Workers. See African Americans; Mini-
    mum wage workers; Women
Wynn, Albert, 101

Zavodny, Madeline, 121, 125, 128

JEROLD WALTMAN is a professor of political science at the University of Southern Mississippi. His publications include *Copying Other Nations' Policies* (1980), *The Political Origins of the U.S. Income Tax* (1985), and *American Government: Politics and Citizenship*, 2d ed. (1999); three coedited volumes, *Dilemmas of Change in British Politics* (1984), *Political Economy: Public Policies in the United States and Britain* (1987), and *The Political Role of Law Courts in Modern Democracies* (1988); and articles on public policy and public law.

Typeset in 10/13 Sabon
with Sabon display
Designed by Dennis Roberts
Composed by Jim Proefrock
at the University of Illinois Press
Manufactured by Versa Press, Inc.

University of Illinois Press
1325 South Oak Street
Champaign, IL 61820-6903
www.press.uillinois.edu